T0159161

VISA
SECRETS
REVEALED

How to Get a Visa to America, Canada, Europe,
Australia and Other Foreign Countries:
Guide to Living and Working Overseas

INTERNATIONAL TRAVEL CONSULTANT

authorHOUSE®

AuthorHouse™
1663 Liberty Drive
Bloomington, IN 47403
www.authorhouse.com
Phone: 1 (800) 839-8640

Published by AuthorHouse 01/24/2019

ISBN: 978-1-5462-7707-1 (sc)
ISBN: 978-1-5462-7712-5 (e)

Print information available on the last page.

DEDICATION

This book is dedicated to Nana Osei, Canada, Emmanuel Kwao Gyesi, Godfred Mensah, Justice Jacobson, Kofi Adzra, George Mensah and GodSon Raynold, aka 'Joe' for their support and encouragement.

INTRODUCTION

Reasons why some people get visas to travel and immigrate overseas and others don't

Let's begin with a few questions: why do some people succeed in getting visas to travel and immigrate to foreign countries the first time they apply, while others try multiple times but are denied? Why are some people able to travel from their native countries to a foreign country, seem to have no problem finding a job, manage to get their 'Green Cards 'in the United States and other forms of permanent resident status in different countries, live there for as long as they want, save most of their earnings and return to their native countries with enough funds to build or buy a brand new house, start a business and live a good life? Why do other people fail when they try to do the same thing? Are some people just lucky? Or do the successful ones know things others don't?

If your goal is to travel from your native country to another country overseas, regardless of the reason or the duration, you are advised to pay close attention to the issues being discussed in this book. You'll find all the answers to the questions that confront people like you, who plan to travel overseas, but are not able to do so for one main reason: their application for a visa has been denied. You're not the only one if you've tried and failed to get a visa to a foreign country or remain skeptical about your chances. The majority of applicants for visas to travel or immigrate to foreign countries are denied, rejected or refused. More than likely you know someone in your community- family member, friend, neighbor- who tried to get a visa and failed.

Let's face it. Visa application denials is the major problem faced by most people when it comes to traveling from one country to another, and more so for those seeking to travel to foreign countries in Europe, America, Australia and other continents from countries in Africa and other areas given the rather dubious geopolitical classification as the "Third World". For the purposes of this discussion, we will define a Third World country as a developing nation, the lowest on the totem pole of country classifications that begins with the First World at the top, followed by the Second World. Most Third World countries are in Africa, Asia and Latin America.

It's the only book of its kind put together with the aim of providing you with the information and insight that, again, people like you, planning to travel overseas from their native countries, or already in a foreign country, need in order to adequately prepare to meet the challenges and problems they would face. The goal is simple: to help you to get the visa you need to travel overseas and also to guide you on how to navigate the rather tricky terrain of living in an overseas country.

Your travel agent will not provide you with this type of information: neither will embassy nor consular officials when you apply for the visa. They will assume you have done your homework and know the basics which includes information you will need to submit an application for a visa. The truth is: it's not their responsibility. The last thing any consular or embassy official would want to do is to advise you on how to get a visa to travel or immigrate to their country.

From this book you will learn what to do right from the beginning, starting with the kind of visa to apply for, how to effectively prepare to submit an application for a visa, how to prepare for the visa interviews, and what to do to be mentally, emotionally and intellectually ready to avoid being intimidated or overwhelmed by the process. It provides you with the kind of information you will need to be able to succeed at every stage of the process.

While it does not necessarily guarantee that anyone who reads this book will succeed in traveling or immigrating overseas, it definitely makes it possible to access the kind of information needed to be able to assess your chances, evaluate the method you're using in your application for a visa, help you to make corrections where you fall short, and ultimately improve your chances of getting a visa to the country of your choice. More importantly, it helps you to really understand what the process is all about, what is involved, and how to prepare to deal with the challenges and problems you will face.

We go one step further. We have included information about life overseas in America, Europe, and Australia and elsewhere along with suggestions on the steps a newly arrived foreigner has to take in order to adjust to the new environment in a foreign country, regardless of how long or short the stay, or the reason for traveling to that particular country.

It is in two parts. Part one focuses on what to do from the beginning. It outlines the complete process, and analyzes why many are denied when they submit applications for visas to foreign countries. We break it down in terms of what is actually involved in preparing to travel or immigrate to a foreign country, what you need to know to be able to make the right decisions about the kind of visa you would need to travel with, how to prepare for the inevitable interview between the applicant and an embassy official who will decide to grant or not grant a visa based on their assessment of the applicant's performance during the interview, and most importantly, how to conduct yourself and the answers to give during the interview.

The second part deals with what to do when you get to the overseas country of your choice and to which you have been given an entry visa. The issues discussed range from how to apply for a visa extension in the case of those who have visitor's visas that may expire before they finish taking care of the business that brought them there, to the fundamental actions to take to avoid becoming an illegal alien or stranded in a foreign country and what to do to make the transition from one status to another.

Again, it is the kind of information you will not get from your travel agent, or find on your own in any book in a library anywhere. It also applies to those desperate enough to use the services of middlemen, the so-called 'connection' people, who seem to be able to get visas for people willing to pay certain sums of money. The more you know about the visa application process, the better off you are in terms of being able to determine if they are capable of delivering on whatever promises they make with respect to getting a visa for you.

Even the overseas embassies don't have that kind of information and won't give it out if they have it. They don't want to make it easy for you to go to their country. It's all here, and all you have to do is to take the time to read it carefully and watch it work for you. We are simply trying to help you to understand that it is not really an impossible task to travel or immigrate to an overseas country. You can make it happen. Others have done it, so can you.

The key is to be prepared to deal with the challenge of

knowing precisely what is involved in the process, what to do to get the visa you need, and how to adjust to the new environment when you get there. And the only way to do it is what we are about to show you.

This international traveler visited Westminster
Abbey when he was in London for a brief visit.
The iconic building and the clock are two of the
most popular tourist attractions in the world.

CHAPTER ONE

Visa Application Process: How it works; documents required; how to prepare for the interview

Applications for visas to various foreign countries are submitted, reviewed, approved, denied or rejected every day all over the world. They are submitted by people seeking permission to travel from their native countries to foreign countries for different reasons. Many are approved; some are denied or rejected, while others may be rescheduled for further review.

All decisions on visa applications are based on information provided on the application forms submitted. Why some succeed and others fail is a question no one can answer. What is commonly known is the importance of providing the right information and the relevant and proper documents to the embassy. The documents and information provided will be used to determine the validity of who you claim to be, the intent and reason why you want to travel to the foreign country in question, and much more.

The key to the entire process is to know and understand the questions being asked on the visa application forms and the absolute necessity to provide the foreign embassy with the right documentation. Some of the documents required are described as mandatory, while others are labeled as supporting documents. We need to clarify what those words mean so you know precisely what we are referring to.

Mandatory documents in the context we are discussing here are documents that contain vital information relating to an individual's identity, financial standing, employment status and other biometric data that they need to confirm identity and statements made on the application forms.

Other documents may not be included in the list of mandatory documents yet play a significant role in the process. These are the supporting documents. It is entirely up to the applicant to decide which documents fall under the supporting documents category. Just bear in mind that every document that contains any kind of information is significant. Not being aware of and not having certain documents may prove to be a problem and a mistake that can potentially lead to the application for a visa being rejected or denied for not having enough relevant information.

The prevention of the mistake of not providing the right documents is what this chapter is all about. Again, our goal is to make you aware of all the documentation needed, the mandatory ones and the supporting documents usually not listed, so you know how to prepare in a way that doesn't miss anything important, and guide you on how to find a way to get them before you go for an interview. Here we go, beginning with the mandatory documents.

MANDATORY DOCUMENTS REQUIRED FOR US VISITOR VISA (Tourist Visa)

It is basically the same process at most foreign embassies when it comes to applying for a visa. For reasons we all

know only too well, majority of applications for foreign travel target the United States, making it the country that receives the most applications and issues the most sought after visa. It is also the most difficult visa to get. We are using the visa application to the US as a model for several reasons, not the least of which is the fact that it is the most popular visa all over the world.

- Original passport with a six month validity beyond expected arrival date in USA.
- All old passports.
- One photograph per specification. Both digital and hard copy of the photograph are required.
- DS160 US Visa application confirmation page stamped at the Visa Application Center (VAC).
- Proof of fee payment, which is a valid receipt.
- Printout of US Interview appointment letter.

Supporting documents for US Visitor Visa (Tourist Visa)

The purpose of supporting documents is to verify -

- Legitimacy.
- Validity.
- Criminal history, if any.
- Financial affordability.
- Intent to return to home country.

Additional documents that support the above mentioned documents help to facilitate a successful visa interview for those who know and prepare for it. Keep in mind that various circumstances warrant different supporting documents. Problem is you have no way of knowing in advance what it is precisely that they might want, so it's best to prepare well in advance and try to get as much documentation as you possibly can, so you don't fall short anywhere.

Following is a list of suggested documents for a few circumstances. The suggested documents are not conclusive and only act as a guide.

Supporting documents for tourism, pleasure, and exploring United States

- Travel itinerary
- Proof of funds (bank statement, copy of passbook, any other proof of cash).
- Tax ID, copy of last year's tax documents.
- Business card, if you have one. If you state anywhere in your application that you are self employed, it becomes necessary to provide the embassy with any documents you have that prove that you are in business.

Supporting documents for visiting children, family, attending family event, etc.

- Letter of invitation from children or relatives or friends.
- Proof of event, invitation card, brochure, etc.

Other suggested documents for visitor visa. Just to be on the safe side, it is suggested that you make sure you obtain every possible document you can think of that can be helpful in providing relevant information about you, the reason why you are planning to travel, and the resources available to you. You want to convince them that

you are totally prepared for the adventure of traveling or immigrating to a foreign country. The following are other documents you should have on you just in case. They might not ask for it, but it's better to be prepared than not.

- Occupation related: If you are employed by a business you don't own, get a letter of employment verification from your boss.
- If you are a government employee, you must get a document stating what organization within the government bureaucracy you work for.
- If you are self-employed, you must get proof of business ownership and financial history. A business card will help in this regard.

REQUIRED DOCUMENTS at the time of Interview.

1. Original Passport + Old Passport.
2. Appointment Letter
3. Confirmation page
4. 2 photos 50 X 50 mm, white background. Normally photos are taken at the time of biometrics only, but it is suggested that you always bring your own photos along with you just in case they have a different system in place.
5. Bank Statements for last 3 months (Personal)
6. Income Tax returns for last 3 years.
7. Salary slips for last 3 months - if employed
8. Company registration proof - if self employed.
9. Retirement Proof - if retired.
10. School / College ID proof
11. Property Papers, Shares, Mutual Funds etc.

Documents from USA if visiting family or friends

1. Passport copy 1st page and last page & visa copy
2. Invitation letter.
3. Accommodation Proof.
4. Bank statements for the last 3 months. (If the trip is being sponsored by an individual or an organization).
5. Salary slips for the last 3 months.
6. Appointment letter.
7. I-134 Affidavit of Support (If the trip is being sponsored by an individual or an organization}

CHAPTER TWO

AT THE INTERVIEW: HOW TO ANSWER QUESTIONS

While it is not possible to predict actual questions that may be asked during the interview, it lies within reason to state that the main purpose of the interview is to determine what is called "Intent" What exactly are you going to the US for? If the question is asked directly, your answer should be direct as well. If it is tourism, family visit, a wedding, a family reunion, etc, state precisely in as few words as possible what it is. As a matter of fact, it's best to say just one word. If it is a wedding, say wedding, no more than is absolutely necessary. If you indicate even slightly that your purpose is anything other than what you stated in your application, you will be denied. That's how it goes. Make sure you don't create the impression that you are going to look for a job, looking for a husband or wife, or that you are going to enroll in school.

Another important area of focus is "Binding Ties" What do you have where you are, in your native country, that you will come back home to? A job, a house, a family? A bank account with money in it would be considered as potentially sufficient proof that you have reason to return, after your visit. Other things will be taken in consideration, of course.

By the time you go for the interview, the consulate officer already knows everything about you. It's in the application forms you submitted to them. They know the answers, from the information and data you provided but he or she wants to see how you answer the questions.

If you indicate to him or her that you do not have the correct 'intent' your application will be denied. There are no two ways about it. If you indicate to him or her in any fashion, directly or indirectly that you may not return to your native country, you will be denied.

Financial statements of the person sponsoring you and statements of your own finances, your property deeds, a letter of employment from your employer, a letter from your bank may be accepted as proof that you have "Binding Ties" that are strong enough to force you to return to your native country.

Most of the documents are not required as part of the application process or the documents the consular official sees, but if you have them at the time of the interview, you might refer to one or two of your papers if things get sticky. In fact, it is quite rare that they ask for and scrutinize all the documents they ask for, but you never know, so don't take any chances and leave out anything.

It has been suggested that it helps to have a round-trip airline ticket as part of the evidence you will be returning. Here again, it is entirely up to the applicant. Just keep in mind that it doesn't make sense to buy an airline ticket for your return when you don't have a visa to go to anywhere, especially if the ticket is not refundable. What about if you are denied and don't get the visa? If you decide to buy a ticket to show at the interview, make sure that it is refundable, just in case.

APPLYING FOR A VISA FOR THE FIRST TIME? HERE ARE SOME HELPFUL HINTS FOR YOU TO INCREASE YOUR CHANCES OF GETTING THE VISA

If you are applying for a visa for the first time, you're advised to not forget for a moment that the odds are against you, that the slightest mistake you make with anything could potentially lead to your application being denied and rejected for a reason that might seem trivial to you, but is substantial enough for them to refuse to approve your application for a visa. You need to be sure of the following:

- Make sure you fill your application form yourself, unless you lack the ability to do so as a result of not understanding the language or inability to write and read in the official language of the country to which you are traveling. Filling out the forms yourself makes it a lot easier for you to remember the information you have provided. Believe it or not, it is possible to forget some of the information that you write, so it's a good idea to revisit the form a few times to familiarize yourself with the information you have written. Never mind the fact that it is all about you. Review it as many times as you possibly can before you go to the interview. If possible, go over your information even as you are waiting to be interviewed.
- Know where exactly you are going to in the foreign country that you have submitted an application for. If it is the United States, make sure you know the correct name of the street, the town or city, the county not the country and the state.

- Know the status of the person inviting you, if the person is not immediate family, is the person a citizen? How did he or she get the citizenship? Was it through the process of being naturalized in the US? If you can get access to the information and know how to do it, it's better to book a hotel/tour itinerary to bring along with you to the interview. if you don't know how to do it, ask others who might know. It's not mandatory, but it sure helps boost your chances.

- Be sure to show very strong ties to and with your home and native country. For example if you are way above 30 years in age and have stated on the form that you are not married with kids, this might be considered to be a red flag. In other words, your whole application becomes questionable and might call for more scrutiny or outright denial.

- You have to be able to provide strong and credible evidence of your employment status. How long have you been working, and hopefully full time? Anything else is a no no. It's a huge plus if you happen to be employed by a reputable and well known organization. The more positive information about your employment status, the better.

- How many other countries have you visited before? They are looking for something to show that you are not new to international travel. Here again, the more information you can provide related to your travel experience outside the confines of your native country, the better. You might also be asked to describe your travel experience.

- You must know how long you intend to stay in the foreign country to which you are traveling and what you plan to do during the period of your visit. How will you spend the days and weeks?

- How much the trip is going to cost compared to your monthly earning. For instance, you cannot be earning $1000 equivalent as monthly gross salary and you want to spend $5000 on a two weeks' vacation. That's like blowing your 5months salary under two weeks. Work with numbers that are logical and make sense.

- Be confident, and lastly, have enough documents with you in case they ask for anything else besides what is listed.

The embassy interview will only last approximately two minutes, from the moment you are at the window until you leave, unless it becomes necessary for the embassy official to discuss or check an issue with other members of the staff or check into facts that are not immediately available. Embassy officials have several interviews a day each. With an 8 hour day, with time deducted for lunch, breaks, and trips to the restroom, that gives them a reasonably decent but sometimes tight schedule. Allow time to call the next person and wait for them, but keep in mind that the time between each interview doesn't leave a lot of time to do anything else but wait for your turn. If all the embassy interviewers are at work on a given day, and there are no problems, they will see everyone. Otherwise, they will speed up to make sure all appointments are seen that day.

Embassy officials interview and screen applicants 5 days a week and have seen and heard everything, from the ridiculous to ignorant to brilliant to concise. But the bottom-line is the information provided, how the applicant carries and presents himself or herself and what kind of luck you have or don't have that moment, that day.

US visa portal clearly states that every visit visa holder is a potential immigrant. Hence, visa approval is for booking your tickets to land in US but not a guarantee to enter the country. It is at the discretion of an immigration officer whether to allow entry or not. at the port of entry.

CHAPTER THREE

Top ten easiest ways to travel, immigrate, move to the United States and the reasons why majority of people try to go there

As improbable as it may seem, traveling or immigrating to the United States is not as difficult as you think, according to travel experts and others who have studied and written about trends and happenings on the subject. If they are to be believed, it's just like traveling or immigrating to any other foreign country. According to them, all you have to do is to submit the required documentation with a visa application and wait for approval. It is that simple. That's how it is supposed to work.

But wait a minute. Is it really that easy to get a visa to America, Europe, Australia and other foreign countries? If so, why do most people complain about how difficult it is to get a visa? Why have most people concluded that getting a visa to travel or immigrate to a country like America is the hardest thing to do?

As far as some people are concerned, it's an impossible task, especially, if you happen to be a native of a Third World country trying to go to a country in the First World. Whether it's true or not is hard to say. But if the conclusion is based on available evidence of how many Africans or other Third World applicants succeed in getting visas to travel or immigrate to America, Europe and Australia and how many get denied, it's easy to understand why people have reached the conclusion that they stand very little or no chance of getting a visa, no matter how hard they try.

Here are some figures that will give you an idea about the fact that people from Third World countries face an uphill battle when they apply for visas to travel or immigrate to a foreign country. According to research undertaken by Schengen, an organization dedicated to studying travel and immigration related issues, 1.5 million people have left sub-Saharan Africa for Europe and the United States since 2010. Millions more continue to make plans to try to find a way to get out. And the figures speak for themselves. They indicate in no uncertain terms that being the native of a Third World country in Africa makes it quite difficult to get a visa to travel or immigrate to most foreign countries, especially America and certain countries in Europe.

The latest report also by Schengen Visa Information published in May 2018 shows that the African countries that recorded the highest number of visa rejections, refusals and denials in the year 2017are the following:

Nigeria

Nigeria tops the list, which comes as no surprise. It is the most populated country in Africa, according to World Meters, an organization that monitors global population trends. The population of Nigeria, as of December 31 2018, was 198,280,587. It was also reported that the rejection rate for visa applications from Nigeria for the year 2017 was 52.5 percent. It means more than half of all applications submitted for visas were denied, for one reason or another. Your guess is as good as mine regarding the reasons for the high rate of visa applications denials for one of the richest and most densely populated countries in Africa.

Libya

9,846 visa applications were submitted from Libya with a refusal rate of 33.3 per cent. Libya's high visa rejection rate is not much of a surprise considering the economic and social hardship in the country that forces many people to flee in search of a better and more stable life in foreign countries.

Democratic Republic of Congo

The Democratic Republic had a refusal rate of 34.8 per cent, a number that will definitely increase with the current political instability in the country that appears to have no end in sight..

Algeria

With a refusal rate of 35.9 per cent, Algeria has one of the highest numbers of visa application refusals in Africa, for a country described in the global media as relatively stable politically, socially and economically.. Morocco's rejection rate is within the same range as Algeria.

Comoros

Even relatively unknown Third World countries appear not to do better with visa application refusals. Comoros, a small island and often forgotten African country had a rejection rate of 36.3 per cent with 4295 applicants in 2017.

Senegal

Senegal, the French-speaking country recorded a total of 69,250 visa applications with a rejection rate of 39.9 per cent

Central African Republic

The landlocked Central African Republic had a rejection rate of 43 per cent.

Guinea

In 2017, Guinea is reported to have had the 3rd highest rejection in Africa with a rejection rate of 43.5 per cent. Out of a population of 12.7 million, 13,432 people applied for a visa to leave Guinea.

Eritrea

With 2,331 applicants in 2017, Eritrea had a rejection rate of 47.8 per cent, indicating that almost 1000, if not a little more, of visa applicants, were rejected.

The above figures represent the reality that the majority of Third World people have to deal with when they apply for a visa to travel or immigrate to a foreign country, especially America. The majority are denied, for one reason or another. You're a very lucky person or you just happen to know precisely what to do to be granted a visa the first time you apply from any African country. That fact is beyond dispute

CHAPTER FOUR

How to qualify for a visa to travel or immigrate to America

Travel experts and others who analyze and write about travel and immigration trends appear to conclude that it is possible for anyone from any part of the world to travel to any foreign country of their choice, so long as they follow certain guidelines and provide proof of their ability to pay for the trip, cover expenses involved, have an idea about what is involved and are prepared to deal with potential problems that may arise. To prove their point, they have put together and made available, hints and guidelines on the proper approach to use in the application for a visa. The following data and information provide details of some of the most important points relating to the factors that may be used as the basis on which to apply for a visa to most foreign countries with the focus on America for reasons that are all too obvious.

Everybody would prefer to go to America when they have an opportunity to choose a foreign country to travel or immigrate to; at least, that is the popular assumption, reinforced to a great extent by the data cited above about the high volume of visa applications to America from African countries and the rejection rate.

The invitation to all to apply for visas can be found in the usual outlets on websites on the Internet. The problem is that they may not be as simple as they seem when it comes to actually applying for and getting the visas to travel or immigrate with. Check it out. You might just be the lucky one. Plus, there is no harm in trying, like they always say. You won't know, if you don't try. You may be the person who can make it happen. The worst that can happen is a rejection, which wouldn't be a surprise.

Let's begin by emphasizing that to qualify for a visa to travel or immigrate to America, the applicant has to meet a number of requirements that have been outlined over the years by the US government in official publications and websites over the years and to which the general public has access. The information and data are not hidden secrets by any stretch of the imagination. Many people from all over the world have successfully used the same information and data to apply for and have been given visas to travel and immigrate to America. You can do the same thing. If others can do it, so can you. The point to keep in mind is that those people did precisely what they were asked to do, beginning with choosing a program they knew they qualified for. Read the following carefully, chose which program fits you and apply for it. Here we go.

1. High End or Needed Skills

If you have high-end professional skills or fall into certain designated groups, you could get a visa from a program titled the EB Series of visas, according to travel experts. The EB visas are basically for those seeking to qualify to be given visas to America on the basis of the skills they have. Possessing those skills increases their chances of being gainfully employed once they enter the country. In other words, they have the potential to make an impact in a useful manner as workers with special skills. This category is for permanent workers and is divided into five subgroups, some of which require a pre-existing job offer from an America based company.

Generally speaking, EB visas are open to people who can demonstrate an excellent level of knowledge and/or significant professional experience in their field, or who simply have skills that the US currently lacks.

2. Regular Job Offer

Even if you don't fall into one of the special categories in the EB visa series, a regular job offer from an American company can get you in the door. In order to get a work visa, your potential employer needs to get a labor certification from the Department of Labor and file a petition for an immigrant worker. The form is one of many that can be obtained from official sources, most of which are explained in detail and can be accessed over the Internet.

Unfortunately, the number of work visas available per year has been dropped to 140,000, and only a certain number of immigrants from each country are accepted. That information is also available online

3. Marriage-Based

If you have an American partner that you intend to marry, he or she can file a US Citizen Petition for a Fiancé to get you to the United States. Be advised that a marriage based application for visa is usually scrutinized by the authorities to make sure it is not faked or forged or not what it claims to be. In other words, it's not easy to get a visa based on a fake or sham marriage. But you have nothing to worry about so long as it is genuine and real.

The basic requirement is that you must have met your potential spouse in person within the last two years. Emphasis is in person. No Internet meeting or anything else will be entertained or accepted. If the petition is accepted, you'll be given a 90-day stay, during which time you need to get married in order to move onto the path towards what is described as a marriage based visa. Again, the authorities are aware of attempts by desperate people to try to file marriage-based visa applications that are not real and have ways and means to find out how legit they are. One thing is for sure. The real marriage-based claims stand a better chance of success, especially if the couple has all the documentation and other information they ask for to make sure it is genuine.

4. The family of a Citizen

If you have immediate family members who are U.S. citizens, you may be eligible for permanent residence. This category only covers parents and children of Americans.

The first step is to have your relative file a Petition for an Alien Relative that will legally establish the relationship between you. Once processed and accepted, you will still need to wait until a visa number becomes available before applying for permanent residence

5. Student

If you're willing to go a roundabout way, starting life in the U.S. as a student is a good option. While there, you'll be able to network with local businesses in your industry – with any luck, you'll graduate with a job offer.

Once you are accepted into one of the programs, you'll be

automatically enrolled in the Student and Exchange Visitor Program and receive a form I-20. This form is required to apply for a student visa. There are two categories of student visa: F-1 is for most academic institutions, and M-1 covers vocational training.

6. Play the Diversity Lottery

For those visa applicants who have tried multiple times to get a visa but were denied for whatever reason, and for those who lack the resources and the financial wherewithal to pay bribes to corrupt government officials and middlemen, there can be nothing better than the Diversity Lottery. Every year 50,000 visas are available for people from countries that have a low number of applications for permanent residence in the United States. This is called the Diversity Immigrant Visa Program, one in which luck is the major component. It's basically like a lottery, and winners get an expedited entry to US citizenship as a result of winning. Unfortunately, you aren't eligible to apply if lots of other people from your home country have already sought permanent U.S. residence, and the results are totally luck-based. Most Third World countries are included in the list.

If you win, you'll be granted an immigrant visa number immediately, making this one of the fastest routes to take. Note that you will be disqualified if you fail to meet minimum education standards or have a criminal record. Try this approach if you consider yourself a lucky person who can win a lottery based visa on nothing else but pure luck. Give it a shot. You have nothing to lose and a whole lot to gain, if luck is on your side.

7. Invest

If you are interested in starting a company in the U.S. or coming on board a new business launched by Americans, you could immigrate as an investor. This visa falls under the EB category for immigrant investors and requires a minimum capital investment of $1 million into a new commercial enterprise.

To qualify, the company must create or preserve permanent full-time jobs for at least 10 U.S. workers. The minimum investment is reduced to $500,000 in rural areas and places experiencing high unemployment. So if you have a million dollars, the gates are wide open for you to walk in as an investor. There are very few visa applicants in this category from Third World countries for obvious reasons.

8. Seek Asylum: Refugees

The United States is open to refugees who are fleeing persecution in their home countries, though now extreme vetting measures have been implemented under President Trump. To qualify you must be able to prove abuses at home and receive a referral to the U.S. Refugee Admissions Program (USRAP).

You may include your spouse and unmarried, minor children in your application. Only limited circumstances allow for other family members. There is no fee to apply for refugee status.

9. Become an Au Pair

If you'd like to stay in the U.S. for a year to check it out and get a sense of other pathways to permanent residence, consider becoming a nanny for an American family.

Technically considered an exchange program, you will

be placed with a family through a Department of State au pair sponsor. Once accepted, you will provide child care in exchange for room and board plus a weekly stipend and up to $500 in education costs. That makes it a great opportunity to take in some schooling, as well.

10. Land an Internship.

If you qualify to take part in a company-sponsored internship program in America, it can open the door for you apply for a visa to travel or immigrate to America in an internship program that has been effectively used by many. If the company you work for has an office in the United States, you may apply to participate in a US-based internship program, if they have one.

If you happen not to qualify for any of the above, don't give up hope. There are a lot more ways besides those outlined here. These are just the officially recognized ways that have been created by the government and used by people who know they qualify based on their qualifications

CHAPTER FIVE

Top 10 easiest methods to use to travel, immigrate, move to Canada

According to travel experts, Canada is a highly sought destination for travelers and immigrants from around the globe, though not the easiest place to travel, immigrate or move to. But it does have well established and reasonable pathways for those willing to put in the work in terms of filling out the appropriate forms, attaching the proper documentation, preparing for and showing up for the interviews.. Once there, you can expect to be welcomed by the locals, who value the strength created by multi-cultural communities. It's worth the effort, energy, time and resources you have to put into making it happen.

Job Transfer

If the company that employs you has a Canada based operation or a subsidiary, you could be eligible for an intra-company transfer to Canada. Called the NAFTA Visa, it is only for people from certain countries that have trade agreements with Canada. The countries include Chile, Jordan, Peru, Colombia,

Liechtenstein, Switzerland, Costa Rica, Mexico, United States of America, Iceland, Norway, Israel, and Panama. This is one of the fastest and easiest ways to make a move to Canada. Problem is the geopolitical dimension of living and working in a country that is a signatory to the NAFTA organization. Unfortunately, only a few countries qualify. We might as well say applicants from Third World countries need not even think about this category. It is just out of reach.

New Job

It is entirely possible to find a new job in Canada and apply for authorization to travel to Canada for the purpose of living and working there. Being gainfully employed by a Canadian company can be used as a perfectly legit basis to apply for and be considered for permanent residency in Canada. The challenge is that the company that offers you a job will have to report to Human Resources and Development in Canada that no Canadian citizen was available to fill the position. This can be quite tricky, but not totally insurmountable. You'll be able to fit in somewhere. And check this out. If you are qualified in one of 347 specified industries for which Canada currently has an employee shortfall, you are eligible for an expedited process called the special entry program. It has been set up to make it a lot easier for those interested in finding jobs and living in Canada. One you qualify to enroll in that program, living and working in Canada will become a reality in no time.

Canada has a lot going for it, both as America's friendly neighbor and in its own right. In fact, Canada consistently ranks near the top of the heap in surveys related to the quality of life. It is also the second largest country in the world but has a low population density, so it's great for people who want a little land around them. You won't miss out on culture, though, with Canada's major cities offering arts and entertainment galore. Ready to go? Try Canada. It's a great country.

Married based visa

Being the spouse of a citizen is one of most foolproof ways to immigrate to travel or immigrate to Canada, as long as the marriage is legit. And they have a system in place to make sure marriage based applications are real, not fake or arranged. The immigration office will be checking in on your relationship for two full years, and if you split with your spouse in that time, you won't be granted permanent residence. So think twice if you are not sure the marriage will last or have any reason to doubt anything.

You may marry your partner either within Canada or in any other country; the process of gaining residency is slightly different if the marriage took place elsewhere. Same-sex marriages are handled the exact same way as heterosexual marriages, provided that gay marriage is legal in the country where the wedding/marriage took place.

Call On a Family Member

If you have a spouse, partner, parent, grandparent, or sibling that is a Canadian citizen, they can sponsor you for permanent residence. If granted, you'll be able to live, work, and/or study in Canada indefinitely.

Part of the deal is that your sponsor agrees to support you financially, if necessary, while you agree to do your very best to support yourself. Since money issues between family members can be touchy, be sure you know what you're getting into, if you go this route.

Go To School

For a roundabout path to permanent residence, consider pursuing higher education in Canada. There are lots of great schools to choose from, but do try and pick one in the province you hope to live in long-term. Usually, you will be required to stay in that province after graduation to work.

A job offer is necessary in order to stay long term in Canada, as already pointed out, but you'll be way ahead of the pack in that regard due to your Canadian education. You can also work part-time during school, but that experience does not count toward any residence streams.

Take a Working Holiday

Relatively young people (between 18-35 years old) are eligible for a working holiday through a program called the International Experience Canada. It allows you to arrive in Canada on an open work permit without a job offer in advance. Really, the only restriction on the type of work you can do on your working holiday relates to strip clubs or escort services. Several countries have an agreement with Canada that facilitates this process. If your country doesn't, don't fret. Canada has several recognized organizations for foreign youth that will help facilitate this visa for a fee. Experience gained through a working holiday can be used toward a later application for permanent residence.

Start a Business

If you are more of an entrepreneurial type, maybe you'd rather start a business in Canada as an alternative to waiting for a company to make a job offer. Canada is currently open for people who have the means and the drive to start businesses that create jobs for Canadians.

Preference is given to businesses that are innovative and can compete on a global scale. If you choose Canada as the location for your new business, you will reap the benefits of low taxes and low business costs in a thriving economy. Bottom-line is; Canada is ready for you if you have the capital to start a business and generate employment.

Seek Asylum

Every year, Canada welcomes approximately 30,000 refugees who have been persecuted in their home countries. There are two systems in place to seek asylum in Canada as a refugee. The Refugee and Humanitarian Resettlement Program works outside of Canada and the In-Canada Refugee Protection Process is for people who have already crossed the border.

The entire process may take up to 18 months, but many potential refugees are given permission to live and work in Canada in the meantime.

Go Through Quebec

Quebec has its own immigration rules and processes that are distinct from the rest of Canada, though largely the same in structure. You can apply to work, study, or marry there.

We suggest that you keep an eye on the Quebec Immigration website as it is updated regularly. To go through Quebec, know that you will need to speak French to have a real shot.

Get Sponsored By a Province

Most of the provinces and territories have a Provincial Nominee Program [PNP], except Quebec, which runs its own immigration process. Just like going through the country-wide process, you'll need marketable skills, a relative who lives there, or the desire to attend school in order to be nominated.

The benefit in following a PNP program is that various provinces are seeking different skills and qualifications, so when you find the place that's a perfect fit, you enter a smaller pool first and have provincial support when you deal with the big guys.

CHAPTER SIX

What kind of visa to apply for to
go to any overseas country

Knowing what kind of visa to apply for is crucial. Believe it or not, some people begin the process of applying for a visa and don't know the type of visa they need for the foreign country they want to travel or immigrate to. They operate on the assumption that all you need to travel or immigrate to a foreign country is any kind of visa. They have no idea what type of visa you need to travel with outside the confines of their native countries. As a result, many are given wrong, sometimes fake visas or visas that expire sooner than they expect and end up as illegal aliens in a foreign country. Worse yet, others find themselves stopped at airports, denied entry, detained and treated like criminals and finally deported.

That is a wrong and dangerous way to get a visa and usually creates very serious problems in most foreign countries for those who enter with just any kind of visa.

Such a mistake can be avoided, by simply doing your homework, beginning with asking questions, just to make sure you know what kind of visa you are getting or will be given to you. Don't be afraid to ask those who know for guidance on what kind of visa to apply for that will make it possible to accomplish the objective you have in mind. Remember, if you don't ask, no one will tell you.

For example, the United States and other countries offer various classes of entry permits to non-citizens. An entry permit is another name for the visa, and the visa basically is a declaration by an official of a foreign country that a native of another country has been authorized to travel or immigrate to their country.

TWO MAIN CLASSES OF VISA ENTRY PERMITS: IMMIGRANT AND NON-IMMIGRANT

There two main classes of visas are immigrant and non-immigrant and they basically mean that one is for those who plan to become an immigrant in a foreign country, while the other is for those who do not plan to stay for a long time in a foreign country. The latter, that is, those with non-immigrant visas will return to their native country, after a brief stay in a foreign country. Immigrant visas have no limitations on how long they want to stay.

We need to clarify something here. The meaning of the word *immigrant* is rife with confusion and ambiguity. It can be easily confused and assumed to represent something else. The questions to which many don't seem to find answers are: who is an immigrant as opposed to an émigré or a migrant? Is the word *immigrant* used solely in reference to foreigners who have resettled in another country? What about people who migrate from one city to another in search of jobs, within a country? What is the difference between immigrants and migrants? Is there a difference between migration and emigration? What about someone who travels overseas just to do business, visit family and friends or seek medical attention?

We will attempt to find answers to some of these questions as we discuss what is involved in the different aspects of international travel and immigration. In the meantime, the following is what governments around the globe say about visas, what the words immigrants and non-immigrants mean in the context of traveling or immigrating to a foreign country in relation to the visa application process.

The official definition of the words immigrant and a non-immigrant, according to various websites, is kind of consistent in most foreign countries. An immigrant is someone from a foreign country who relocates to live in another country. They may or may not be citizens.

Non-immigrants travel or move to another country on their own volition for a certain duration but not permanently. They are subject to the laws of their adopted country and may be allowed into an overseas country if they have work or a place to live. Proper documentation from the authorities is required to show that no laws have been broken and that the individual involved has complied with all the rules and regulations.

A website which disseminates information on matters relating to the visa application process for people seeking to travel to the United States says that the same two types of visas are given to those traveling or immigrating to America. They are the immigrant and non-immigrant visa. Most foreign countries have similar classifications and two kinds of visa entry permits, the immigrant visa, and the non immigrant visa. .

Again, an immigrant visa to the United States is a permanent visa, meaning it authorizes you to stay for an extended period of time. It is issued to people who are granted U.S. permanent residency (Green Card status). It means that the Green Card permits you to live in America as a permanent citizen.

Immigrant visas are issued through family relationships, employment and refugee programs, to name a few. There are other classes. According to the website, there are 32 categories of immigrant visas. It doesn't break it down in terms of what the immigrant visa classifications are.

It emphasizes that a non-immigrant visa is a temporary visa and is issued to people who plan to be in the U.S. for a short period of time. Non-immigrant visas are issued for tourism, medical treatment, business, temporary work or study, for example. There are 20 categories of non- immigrant visas, and again, it doesn't list what those classifications are.

It goes on to explain the immigrant visa process and how to get a Green Card for those interested in living in America for an extended period. All the information is available on the government website and can be easily accessed on the Internet.

HOW TO APPLY FOR AN IMMIGRANT VISA, ALSO KNOWN AS THE GREEN CARD

According to the website, people seeking to immigrate to America may apply for a U.S. Green Card through consular processing. An overview of that process is outlined in greater detail elsewhere in this book but summarized here as the following:

First, you have to find your Green Card category among the 32 classifications. You can apply for a Green Card through family, employment, a special class, or a humanitarian program.

File an immigrant petition.

In most cases, you will need an immigrant petition as the first step of the process.

Generally, this application is completed by a U.S. sponsor, such as a relative or employer, and filed on your behalf with the USCIS, the immigration authorities.

Wait for the decision on your petition.

The USCIS will notify the petitioner when the application is approved.

Wait for a notification from the National Visa Center.

The USCIS will send your approved petition to the Department of State's National Visa Center where it will remain until an immigrant visa number is available. The National Visa Center will notify you when the petition is received when a visa number is available, and when to submit visa processing fees and supporting documentation.

Go to your visa interview.

All visa applicants must attend an interview at a U.S. embassy or consulate. Ultimately, this is where the decision on your application is made.

Get your immigrant visa and travel to the U.S.

If your application is approved, you will be granted an immigrant visa and a "Visa Packet".

This packet is to be given to Customs and Border Patrol upon entering the U.S.

Receive your Green Card.

Once you are in the U.S., you will receive your Green Card by mail.

THE NON IMMIGRANT VISA PROCESS

The Non-immigrant Visa Process; how it works

Here are the steps to get a temporary, non-immigrant U.S. visa.

Find your visa category.

There are several non-immigrant visa categories, including tourism, business, study, and work.

Complete the DS-160, Online Non-immigrant Visa Application.

This is an online application available on the US Department of State website.

Schedule a visa interview

All applicants must attend an interview at the U.S. embassy or consulate near you. There you will be interviewed for country-specific questions.

Pay the visa application processing fee.

Get your visa and travel to the U.S

CHAPTER SEVEN

How to prepare to submit an application for a visa to any overseas country

Appearing at an embassy to be interviewed by a consular officer is the grand finale of a series of steps required by both the native country and the country to which one plans to travel or immigrate. These steps include having a current passport. A passport is the only document that shows officials of the embassy of the country you plan to travel or immigrate to that you can leave your native country, to begin with. A passport basically proves beyond doubt that you are the person you claim to be.

Without a passport, it is not possible to travel anywhere. It is recognized globally as the most reliable form of personal identification for citizens when the need arises to prove one's nationality. In addition to a passport, students or those planning to pursue higher education in foreign countries have to produce letters of admission to colleges and universities, affidavits and letters of support from sponsors stating their willingness and ability to come up with the funds needed to pay tuition and other costs.

Visitors or others claiming to be traveling to a foreign country for a short period of time to do business, visit friends or seek medical attention have to convince consular officers they plan to return to their countries. They want to make sure that applicants for visitor's visas are not using the visit mainly for the purpose of gaining entry into a foreign country with plans to stay there after the visa expires. That would make them illegal aliens, but they know too that many don't care about being illegal and would use any means necessary to get a visa to travel to a foreign country.

Those who declare their intention to immigrate or travel to a foreign country have to meet some seriously stringent requirements for obvious reasons. They want to make sure you know what is involved in the process and won't end up as a liability in their country. In other words, you won't become an illegal alien in their country.

IT ALL BEGINS WITH A PASSPORT

Ordinarily, obtaining a passport is supposed to be a simple process. In most countries, a passport is one of the most popular and common government documents issued to those who want to travel beyond the borders of the country in which they were born. All you have to do is fill out an application, submit it to the appropriate authorities and wait for the passport to be issued. It's supposed to be that simple and straightforward.

This is how it works in the United States, and in other countries around the world. Not so in a lot of developing countries, particularly in Africa. In countries such as Ghana, Nigeria, and others in East, North and South Africa, obtaining a passport has become a highly complicated process. Government regulations, bureaucratic red tape, and bribery and corruption have transformed what is supposed to be a very simple process into a mind-boggling, complicated, secretive process, featuring government officials demanding bribes, middlemen who have to be paid, exceedingly high government imposed fees and many other factors.

WHEN GETTING A PASSPORT IS NOT EASY

So difficult and complicated is the process that most people seeking passports find themselves intimidated by the prospect of dealing with the hassle of trying to get it on their own and have to enlist the services of middlemen. The middlemen know of the problems to be encountered by the uninitiated, and those who attempt to secure a passport on their own. They know that passport application files can disappear, or simply can't be traced, that government workers who are supposed to process the passport applications suddenly become indisposed and are not available for weeks or months on end. The result is a process which takes days in other countries becomes a long and protracted affair that can drag on for months.

ROLE OF MIDDLEMEN: ARE THE 'CONNECTION PEOPLE' THE ANSWER TO SOLVING PASSPORT AND VISA PROBLEMS?

Consequently, the role of the middlemen has become increasingly significant, even inevitable. It has become part of the process, more or less. Quite often, the only way to get a passport in some countries in many Third World countries is to pay a middleman, who in turn, pays somebody else. Somehow it works and many passports and visas are obtained this way.

How? It is a closely guarded secret, but the general idea is that it consists of a network of people who have access to those in charge of issuing the passports. The middlemen intercede on behalf of their clients; pay bribes or do other favors, get their cut and the passport is issued. However, this is just the beginning. The real challenge is to get the visa for the country to which one plans to travel or immigrate.

THIRD WORLD VISA APPLICANTS KNOWN TO HAVE A DIFFICULT TIME GETTING APPROVALS FOR VISA APPLICATIONS?

Again, the process is not as easy as it sounds, at least not for people from developing countries in the Third World. The odds are stacked against them, or so it seems, for various reasons. The majority have no idea about the immigration process, besides their desire to leave their native countries, which doesn't exactly make a strong case for anyone to be considered for a visa to travel anywhere.

This means most applicants from Third World countries don't qualify to begin with because they have little or nothing in the form of material possessions or wealth. It makes it very difficult and, quite often impossible, for many people in some countries in Africa to get a visa on their own to countries such as the United States, England, and Canada.

According to information on websites of most foreign countries, the official channels are open to anyone who qualifies to apply for a visa. There is supposed to be no discrimination on the basis of color, religion, race, nationality or economic status. In theory, that is. In practice, it is a totally different story. Obtaining a visa in the developing countries, particularly in some parts of Africa is seen by many as the most difficult undertaking to be faced by any individual planning to immigrate or travel to a foreign country.

HOW THE PROCESS WORKS

The interview session at most foreign embassies has all the characteristics of legal proceedings of sorts with the applicant playing the role of the defendant and the consular officers playing the role of the judge. The burden of proof lies with the applicants. They are required to prove beyond doubt that they mean what they say and can back it up with documentation that corroborates what they say, if required. And most of the time, they require documents as proof.

If you appear before a consular officer and ask to be given a visitor's visa to the United States, for instance, you have to provide evidence of your economic status in your country to counter the presumption that you may be using that as a ploy just to leave your native country. You have to show documentary evidence of wealth or property, marital and family status, employment history or entrepreneurial background and accomplishments and an established bank account containing considerable amounts of funds. It cannot be a dormant account either with one lump sum recently deposited. They look for bank accounts that appear to be active with regular withdrawals and deposits and other activities that indicate frequent use of funds in the account.

You have to convince the interviewing officer that you have every reason to return to your country. Failure to do that automatically disqualifies the applicant.

Only a few succeed in securing a visa and end up boarding planes for America, Europe or Australia, or other European countries. So complicated is the process that many simply get intimidated, fail to make a strong and coherent presentation or simply just mess up and don't get the visa as a result. Those not willing or afraid to go through the process themselves sometimes seek the services of intermediaries, who manage to circumvent the process by way of either forgery or manipulation of information or outright bribery.

On the other hand, those who can afford it have at their disposal legal firms and consultants who specialize in providing assistance to people planning to travel or immigrate to a foreign country. The Internet advertises services of firms that will help you to immigrate to Australia, Canada, Germany, and other countries. For a fee, they will advise on how to invest funds in foreign countries, and how to leverage investment to gain permanent residence, etc.

CHAPTER EIGHT

Reasons people immigrate or travel overseas

It has been argued that it is part of human nature to want to travel or immigrate. After living in a particular place for a period of time, the desire to move usually kicks in. Some people ignore it or just refuse to recognize it and don't do anything about it. Others take it seriously and make moves that lead to going somewhere else. For those who decide to act on the impulse to move, and change their environment as a result, there is always a reason, or better yet, they find a reason to justify making the move.

Travel experts and writers have observed the trends, analyzed various factors and have come out with reasons that explain why people travel or immigrate to other countries. Check it out and see if they are right. You might just find out that they know more than you think. According to travel experts and writers, people travel or immigrate because of the following reasons.

Escaping Conflict

Escaping conflict areas seems to be a leading cause for people who leave their native countries to travel or immigrate overseas either for short or long term stays. As already mentioned in another chapter, no one can be blamed for making a decision to travel or immigrate from an unsafe country to a foreign country where they would feel more secure and safe and don't have to worry about dealing with life threatening situations. Anyone in their right mind and able to do so will chose that option. Political ideologies and cultural conflicts in many countries in some parts of the Middle East, Africa, and other developing countries often force people to leave their native countries. The majority make every effort to go to developed countries in North America and Europe, hoping to live in a safer environment where they can pursue higher education, start businesses or find stable and better paying jobs.

Environmental Factors

Storms, floods, tsunamis, and several other natural disasters create the need or force people to flee and seek asylum in other countries considered to be relatively safer than where they are. Here again, it makes perfect sense to go somewhere else if your present circumstances are not safe for reasons that are fundamentally environmental.

Escaping Poverty

Described as economic immigrants, lots of people travel from their native countries to foreign countries in search of better paying jobs that will make it possible for them to earn and save money, or pursue educational opportunities that will prepare them to get better paying jobs, live in modern and advanced housing facilities; in brief, enjoy a better quality of life as a result of living in a country where the standard of living is high.

Higher Education

As alluded to above, one of the major reasons people travel or immigrate to foreign countries, especially the younger generation, is the pursuit of higher education. They have made the decision that they stand a better chance of pursuing higher education in a foreign country and may even get a better job as a result.

Love

The internet has ushered in a totally new dimension to life, especially as it relates to personal and social relationships. It is capable of bringing people closer together emotionally and in a way that has not been possible before. There have been several instances where people travel great distances to be with their loved ones as a result of having met and interacted on the Internet. This is a new and exciting world of limitless opportunities and the adventurous ones are not missing out on the fun. Not for the faint hearted, though.

Family Influences

Most families in the majority of Third World countries usually have a family member or know someone who has experienced life overseas in a foreign country and has returned home with enough funds to build a nice house, start a business and still be able to live a reasonably decent lifestyle. Others return home to visit for a short time, but bring enough dollars, Euros or francs to be able to 'live large' spend lots of money, have big fun and generally live a lifestyle they wouldn't have been able to if they hadn't traveled or immigrated to a foreign country. They help perpetuate and reinforce the notion that going overseas solves people's problems. Not necessarily true, but it's not easy to convince desperate people that they have wrong ideas about life overseas when they see such things.

Better Healthcare

It is an open secret in most Third World countries that those who can afford it travel overseas to get medical attention whenever the need arises for special medical attention. It is also known that only a few can afford that luxury. By the same token, they are aware that the kind of medical care they get overseas is usually accessible to the majority of the people who live and work there. In other words, you don't have to be a rich person to get decent medical attention when you live in a developed country, as opposed to not getting any medical care in a poor underdeveloped Third World country where there are no hospitals to go to. They feel the need to get the best possible healthcare for themselves and their families. Simply stated, some people travel or immigrate to foreign countries in search of better healthcare.

Nature

It is not common among Third World people, but it is known that many people shift their entire lives at some point, leaving their old life behind just so they can live the kind of lifestyle that suits them. Regardless of what it takes, what is involved or even what it is, some people would go to great lengths to travel or immigrate to foreign countries in search of what they consider to be ideal for them in their quest for what makes them happy. It happens more frequently than you know.

While the reasons to move may seem different, at the end of the day, traveling or immigrating to a foreign country, for whatever reason, is almost always a way to improve the life you currently live.

HELPFUL HINTS ON HOW TO PREPARE TO TRAVEL OVERSEAS AND THE COMMON MISTAKES TO AVOID

- The most difficult and stressful part of the process of traveling to or immigrating to an overseas country is getting a passport that allows you to leave your country and a visa that authorizes you to enter an overseas country. Third World people experience more stress and frustration as a result of knowing that they have little or no chance of getting a visa. More than likely, their visa appiications will be denied, for one reason or the other. Reading this will prepare you to avoid the frustration and agony of denials and rejections.

- As pointed out above, most applicants for visas for foreign countries from Third World countries and other developing countries are denied when they apply for a visa to travel to an overseas country the first time. The high volume of visa denials for people from Africa and other developing countries has been blamed on their inability to produce documents needed to verify certain things such as finances, marital status, educational credentials, bank accounts, etc. Whether it is true or not that majority of Third World applicants fail to meet the requirements as a result of their inability to produce proper documents is a question that cannot be easily answered. What is undeniable is the fact that majority get denied the first time they apply. The key is to know what is involved in the process and what documents are actually required.

- It is assumed that most people from the Third World that decide to travel to foreign countries to find work, save money and come back home to live a better life. While that may apply to many visa applicants from Third World countries, it is also true that many travel overseas to do business or visit family and friends with no intention of staying. Problem is, it's not easy to convince the visa granting authorities when it comes to making a case that an application for a visitor's visa to visit somebody or to do business is in reality, what is being sought.

CHAPTER NINE

How to prepare to travel to an overseas country for a short or a long stay

Some of the major problems faced by most Third World people who plan to travel overseas are the following: their inability, hesitancy or unwillingness to provide required documentation and failing to provide correct answers to questions during the visa interview. Not knowing how to explain the reason why they are applying for the visa and not having enough relevant information about the country to which they are traveling seem to be their major flaws. They simply conclude that all they have to do is buy an airline ticket, get some kind of a visa by any means necessary, board a plane and fly to their chosen destination in a foreign country. Never mind, if they know little or nothing about the political, economic, social and racial systems they would have to deal with if they succeed in getting a visa to travel or immigrate to that foreign country. They consider those issues as the least of their problems.

That translates into not being adequately prepared to deal with the challenges and problems they will face during the process of applying for the visa. As a result, they make many serious mistakes right from the beginning. Such mistakes include applying for the wrong type of visa, or being given a fake visa by middlemen or 'connection' people, traveling at the wrong time such as in the middle of winter without warm clothing, not finding relatives and friends, running out of funds and not getting any help from people and other sources they think will help them with things like room and board. Anyone who has experienced one of those situations knows how serious and traumatic life can be for the victims

Most people can avoid such problems if they do one thing; prepare well, beginning with researching and getting the right information about the visa application process and the country to which they plan to travel or immigrate. Unfortunately, most don't. Until recently, the majority of people, especially those from developing countries in Africa, and elsewhere who travel to Europe, the United States, and other places, had the tendency to know little or nothing about what is really involved in the process of travelling or immigrating from one country to another. To many, especially those bent on leaving their native countries by any means necessary, it was simply a matter of putting the funds together to be able to buy a ticket, figure out a way to get a visa to the country of their choice, board a plane and fly out, and hope for the best.

Even those who have made up their minds to travel outside the confines of their country as immigrants and are ready to make an effort to go through the rather difficult process of applying for an immigrant visa appear to have a similar mindset. Very little time, effort and energy is put into seeking information about the process and the foreign country they plan to travel or immigrate to.

MANY PEOPLE DON'T MAKE THE EFFORT TO LEARN ABOUT THE COUNTRY THEY WANT TO TRAVEL OR IMMIGRATE TO

As alluded to above, having some knowledge about the country to which they are traveling or immigrating is not considered to be necessary, or even useful. Indeed, seeking information about foreign countries isn't a priority for the majority of people from Third World countries planning to travel overseas for business, tourism, or as prospective immigrants. It's all about getting out of their country as fast and as hassle-free as possible. The reason is simple: they are really not too concerned about the fact that they may know little or nothing about the country to which they seek or have gotten a visa to travel or immigrate to. They have made up their minds that regardless of what the issues may be, they would be ready to face and overcome them when the time comes. They just want to get there by whatever means they can find and deal with the issues later, whatever they may be.

"The last thing anyone from the Third World will think about is learning about a country overseas, besides what they already know from books, magazines, and movies. They look at that as the least of their problems; they want to get out and that's all that matters, at that point," says Verna Davis, an American who visited the Ivory Coast and Ghana in the early nineties.

THE RIGHT WAY TO PREPARE TO TRAVEL OR IMMIGRATE OVERSEAS BEGINS WITH KNOWING ABOUT THE COUNTRY YOU WANT TO TRAVEL TO

The point being made is this: having limited or no information and knowledge about the country they travel or immigrate to means not being adequately prepared. As a result, most are not in a position to know what to expect and how to deal with the problems and challenges that are faced by anyone who decides to travel to a foreign country. No matter who you are or where you come from, there are legal, social, economic, financial and quite often, political changes one has to go through in order to be able to travel to any overseas country and to be able to continue to live there once you have gained entry.

Again, the recurring theme in these discussions is the fact that most people in developing countries are misinformed about the process of traveling aboard and the immigrant life overseas. They don't know what it's all about and make no effort to educate themselves or get the relevant information needed in order to be better prepared to cope with applying for a visa and living abroad. Regardless of how long or short the stay in a foreign country, it is absolutely necessary to prepare to deal with it in more ways than one. We repeat: one way to prepare is to know as much as you possibly can about the country to which you are traveling.

However, it is evident that the majority of travelers and immigrants from developing countries don't know what to expect in a foreign country in terms of the problems they might have to face, or the changes they have to go through once they arrive in a foreign country. It includes those who have made plans to travel abroad and live there for an extended period as students or immigrants. For example, many have no idea that as a foreigner in most overseas countries, your status is similar to that of a second-class citizen. They don't know that there is a lot of bureaucratic red tape to go through in order to continue to reside legally in the country of choice, that deportation and other forms of harassment are often used to control the movement of foreigners.

IT'S A BIG MISTAKE TO HAVE LITTLE OR NO KNOWLEDGE ABOUT THE OVERSEAS COUNTRY TO WHICH YOU'RE TRAVELING.

The question becomes: why do people, particularly prospective immigrants, from Third World countries seem not to be too concerned about not having enough knowledge and information about the immigration process?

And the answer is: they are not interested in knowing about the problems involved. That will be an honest answer. So compelling is the desire to travel overseas, to get out of their native country by any means necessary, or to immigrate and stay away for as long as they possibly can that everything else doesn't really matter. They assume that whatever happens in the process can be dealt with. The important thing, as far as they are concerned, at that moment, is to find a way to get out.

No matter how daunting life is alleged to be in a foreign country, to someone about to experience it anew, they're ready to deal with it. Nothing can stop them. Such a determined person from any Third World country who has made up his or her mind to leave their native country to go overseas will try to do so regardless of how dangerous or problematic the journey would be. They simply operate on the assumption that he or she would manage to survive. All they need to do is to gain entry to a foreign country and the rest would take care of itself. As far as they are concerned, their determination is an adequate substitute for knowledge, preparedness, and expertise. They also expect to be able to work or go to school immediately when they manage to get out and gain entry into a foreign country

Wrong. Wrong. Wrong. Like everything else, traveling overseas for whatever reason has to be undertaken by people who are prepared in more ways than one. Problem is: it's not easy, impossible really, to try to convince a desperate man or woman bent on traveling or immigrating overseas from a Third World country to embrace the notion that life overseas is less rewarding or glorifying than they think it is. Once their minds are made up, nothing can change it, it seems. What they don't know is that the laws and regulations governing immigration tend to have very strict guidelines relating to employment for the immigrant. Sheer determination isn't enough.

Not surprisingly, many people from developing countries end up having a lot of problems after they have travelled or immigrated to countries in North America, Europe, etc, as a result of their unpreparedness and willingness to risk everything. They end up as illegal immigrants, becoming part of a problem of illegal immigration that haunts most countries around the world with sizeable populations of immigrants

The most important question is: how do you go about getting the visa to the country of your choice? Along with it are other equally important and pressing questions that will help you to decide the kind of visa to apply for. They include the following: how long do you plan to stay in the foreign country you're traveling to? What kind of resources do you have? Is it a brief business visit or do you plan to stay for a while in that country and if so, what kind of financial and other resources do you have that can take care of room and board and other needs?

MAKE THE EFFORT: SOURCES OF INFORMATION AVAILABLE ALL OVER THE INTERNET

Try as much as you possibly can not to convince yourself that all you need is any kind of visa that will make it possible to gain entry into any country overseas. Many have done just that and encountered serious problems. They found out the mistake they had made only after they gained entry into foreign countries and realized what they had gotten themselves into. Nothing but problems leading to becoming illegal in a foreign country.

For instance, if your intention is to travel and stay for an extended period as an immigrant, that option is open to anyone who has the means and the resources. There is still a certain degree of risk involved. It is not guaranteed that you will get an immigrant visa even if you do everything right. .But the key is to apply for and try to get the right type of visa that gives you enough time to begin the process of changing your status to become a permanent resident when you get there, if that is your intention.

If you are desperate enough to take the risk to ask for and get a visitor's visa with a plan to convert later, you should bear in mind that it would not be easy for you to change your status when you get there. It is a long and complicated process in every foreign country, especially if you are from a Third World country. The important thing is that it is not impossible to change one's status from visitor to immigrant. What many people don't know is how difficult, expensive and frustrating it is or can be. But it can be done.

It is also common knowledge that in most Third World countries there are 'connection' men and so-called agents and middlemen who specialize in securing visas for those willing to pay huge amounts of money. Problem is: they are limited in what they can do and usually can only get visitor's visas for their clients that expire after a short time. They don't provide much of anything else. All they want is your cash. And sometimes they only can get fake visas that can get you into a lot of trouble.

The most dangerous aspect of the 'connection' arrangement

and securing visas from unofficial sources is this; they won't tell you that once your visa expires, you will become an illegal alien in the foreign country to which have gained access as a visitor. Neither will they be able to get you any kind of documentation that will help you to get a job or go to school in any foreign country. You don't want to do that. Avoid such a visa, at all costs, if you can.

THE RIGHT WAY TO APPLY FOR A VISA TO AN OVERSEAS COUNTRY

Rule number one: Find out as much information and data as possible about the country you plan to travel or immigrate to. It is imperative that you know a whole lot about the country you plan to travel or immigrate to. The embassy official who will interview you and grant or deny you a visa will expect you to have some basic information about the country you want to travel to.

Make a decision regarding how you want to go about applying for a visa. As indicated elsewhere, you have a number of options. You can apply for the visa yourself, use the services of an agent, pay a travel agent, or for the desperate ones, pay a smuggler or a 'connection' person to get you into that country with a visa that makes it possible to gain entry and nothing else. The real problem is how to get the proper visa you need or in the case of those who seek the help of others, how to find the right person to help you get the right visa.

Rule number two: Make sure you know what documents they want to see. Usually, they would want to see the following documents for those applying for a visa; passport, a bank statement showing that you have a fairly reasonable amount of money in the bank, evidence of your marital status, and a deed to a house if you have one in your name. The embassy officials will expect you to convince them that you have reasons to return to your country. For students, they want to see a letter of admission, a statement of support from the person sponsoring you or who will be responsible for paying your fees, provide room and board, etc.

For those seeking a visa to go overseas to do business, seek medical attention, visit family or friends, the onus is on them to prove that they are not using the visa for any other purpose other than what is stated on the application. Those applying for business purposes have to show they are legit business people. It is absolutely necessary to have documentation that shows that you are really in business. The documents have to consist of every official certification from the appropriate authorities showing that you have a business that is registered and actively doing business, paying taxes and is in compliance with all the rules and regulations of the land.

When all these fail, there's a last option that is open only to those interested in going to the United States; you can try your luck on the immigration lottery visa. It's free. All you need is access to the Internet.

These are the most common mistakes most immigrants make in the beginning.

- Not knowing beforehand what they would have to do to be able to live legally in the countries to which they travel or immigrate.
- Assuming relatives and friends would help them when they encounter problems. Immigrants, especially those newly arrived; often don't know that they cannot expect to get much help from fellow immigrants,

sometimes even when they are related to each other. They might share the knowledge and experience of the immigration process they may have gathered over the years about life in that particular country. It might end right there. This kind of information might be helpful in finding jobs, housing, etc. Unlike back home in their native countries where family members and friends are almost always ready to help out, immigrants who live in foreign countries quickly pick up the habit of not allowing themselves to be put into situations where they have to spend time, energy and effort that directly benefit someone else, regardless of who that person happens to be. Their time and resources become precious commodities they use mostly to their own benefit. It is a lifestyle that is completely different from what most people know from Third World cultures. They act in what might seem to be a selfish manner because they know their own survival, and quite often, their success in overseas countries depend on how they use both their time and resources

- Underestimating the gravity of the problems they would face as immigrants when it comes to changing their status from student or visitor to permanent resident, etc

HELPFUL HINTS FOR BOTH NON-IMMIGRANT AND IMMIGRANT VISA APPLICANTS

- Do your homework.
- Get the right kind of entry permits. Make sure you get the right kind of visa you need that will make it possible to have enough time to accomplish all the objectives you have in mind. If it is at all possible, try to avoid the risk of traveling without the appropriate visa.
- Don't make the mistake of assuming that things will work out once you have left your native country. Don't make the mistake of assuming that family members and friends already overseas will help you in times of need or trouble. They have their own problems and priorities and may not be able to help you.
- Make sure you know what to expect. You can do this by talking to those who have already experienced overseas travel and immigration and related activities and insist they tell you about the downside as a well as the upside.
- Don't make hasty decisions, and don't try to rush the process.

CHAPTER TEN

Why visa applications to America, Europe, Canada, and Australia from people from Third World countries often get denied

The real challenge is to get a visa for the country to which one plans to travel or immigrate to. Again, the process is not easy by any means, at least, not for people from developing countries in Africa and other parts of the Third World. The odds are stacked against them, for various reasons we have already explained elsewhere.

No wonder many people from different African countries often make the decision not to even try to get a visa and take the risk of crossing the Sahara Desert or try other dangerous and risky ways to get to countries and places where they hope to sneak to Europe or America through the back door.

Many suffer tragic deaths. They get lost and die of thirst or hunger in the desert or are drowned when the boats in which they are being smuggled across the Mediterranean sink for one reason or another. Pictures of dead bodies of African and other Third World immigrants being recovered from the seas and deserts are quite common on the global television these days.

One of the main problems is that the majority have no idea of what is actually involved in traveling overseas and the immigration process, besides their desire to leave their native countries. And that doesn't exactly make a strong case for anyone applying to be considered for a visa to travel anywhere unless they happen to have accumulated considerable wealth in their native countries they intend to invest and can provide documented proof.

This means most applicants from Third World countries don't qualify to begin with because they have little or nothing in the form of material possessions or wealth. This makes it very difficult, if not impossible for visa applicants in countries in Africa and other developing countries to get a visa on their own to countries such as the United States, England, and Canada and elsewhere.

IS IT A LEVEL PLAYING FIELD WHEN IT COMES TO GETTING A VISA TO NORTH AMERICA, EUROPE, AUSTRALIA, etc.?

Getting a visa to travel to any country overseas is supposed to be a very simple and routine process. The United States Consular Offices websites outline the visa requirements in simple English. Applicants are advised on what they have to do to get a visa: numbers to call or websites to go to make an appointment, documents to bring, and schedules of working hours of the consulate. Most importantly, you are reminded that you get a second chance, if the first attempt doesn't succeed.

They also encourage you to believe that anyone who qualifies will be granted a visa, that absolutely no one is disqualified to submit an application for a visa. The popular assumption is that no one is subjected to any form of discrimination on the basis of color, religion, race, nationality, financial and economic status. In theory, that is. In practice, it is a totally different story. Obtaining a visa in the developing countries, particularly in some parts of Africa, has become by far the most difficult undertaking to be faced by any individual planning to travel to North America, Europe, Australia, and Canada as students, visitors reconnecting with family and friends on for business purposes. It's even more difficult when applying as an immigrant.

GO TO THE VISA INTERVIEW WELL PREPARED. MAKE SURE YOU HAVE ALL THE DOCUMENTS REQUIRED. HAVE AN IDEA ABOUT THE QUESTIONS THEY WILL ASK.

The interview session with most foreign embassy officials has all the characteristics of legal proceedings of sorts with the applicant playing the role of the defendant and the consular officers playing the role of a judge. The burden of proof lies with the applicants. Applicants are required to prove beyond any reasonable doubt that they are telling the truth and can back it up with documentary proof if required.

If you appear before a consular officer and ask to be given a visitor's visa to the United States, for instance, you have to provide evidence of your economic status in your country to counter the presumption that you may be using that as a ploy just to leave your native country. You have to show documentary evidence of wealth or property, marital and family status, employment history or entrepreneurial background and accomplishments and an established bank account containing considerable amounts of cash. You have to convince the interviewing officer that you have every reason to return to your country. Failure to do that automatically disqualifies the applicant. And the only way to succeed in convincing the consular official is to show confidence, and the ability to give the right answers to the questions asked. Next question is how do you know what questions will be asked? The answer is simply this; they want to know why you want a visa to go overseas, whether you really intend to return to your native country if you have applied for a visitor's visa and whether you are who you claim to be.

The problem is the majority fail to meet the requirements and their visa applications are denied for that particular reason. Again, it's easy to explain why most visa applicants are denied for not having the proper documents, when they make their initial appearance at most foreign embassies to apply for entry visas.

In most Third World communities and cultures, legal and official documents are not very common. Many, especially those with minimal or no education, have no idea what a bank statement is, or don't have bank accounts, to begin with. Therefore qualifying to be interviewed on the basis of documents provided such as a bank statement can become a huge problem.

To make matters worse, all documents that have to be obtained are just as difficult to get, no matter where they are processed, be it a government department or a private company. You are just as likely to be frustrated by governmental bureaucratic red tape as by corrupt bank officials who just don't want to take the time and trouble to locate the documents or demand bribes before they do their job. Either way, it doesn't make it easy to get documents of any kind in many Third World communities.

YOU CANNOT BRIBE, SWEETTALK OR FAST TALK YOUR WAY INTO GETTING A VISA TO AMERICA, CANADA, AUSTRALIA OR ELSEWHERE. YOU HAVE TO EARN IT

Another significant factor is the assumption within the general population in most Third World countries that you cannot bribe the visa issuing officials of European and North American embassies or use any other means to influence them to give you a visa when you don't qualify as a result of not being able to provide documentary proof to support the claims made in an application. The perception is that no amount of bribes or pressure from top officials seems to work, at least, everyone knows for a certainty that you cannot walk up to an American or a European diplomat and hand over an envelope containing cash as a bribe and expect not to be arrested. So the general feeling is that the right thing to do is to submit the required documents, provide the right answers during the interview and you are just as likely to be given a visa like anyone else in any part of the world.

Again, the general public in most developing countries operate on the assumption that American and European diplomats and embassy officials are not prone to being bribed, and don't even try to do or say anything that would suggest an attempt to bribe, corrupt or compromise them in any way. Whether it is true or not has not been raised as a matter of public debate, partly because of the continued and consistent effectiveness with which most foreign embassy officials handle the business of issuing visas around the world. They have proven in no uncertain terms they are not easy to influence in ways that will compromise their ability to perform their duties effectively and objectively. Their approach to decision making with regard to who gets or is denied a visa is generally described as fair and based solely on criteria outlined by their governments. The process places emphasis on information provided by applicants as well as the demeanor and performance of the applicant during the interview.

CONSULAR OFFICIALS CANNOT BE EASILY FOOLED, BRIBED OR MANIPULATED. YOU HAVE TO GIVE THEM WHAT THEY ASK FOR AND GIVE THE RIGHT ANSWERS

It is also suspected that consular officers are trained to spot and interpret subtle as well as obvious signs of inconsistencies in answers given to questions and the attitude of the applicants during the process, to the degree where most applicants who make an appearance before them know in advance that the embassy officials can detect when a lie is being told or when information provided is less than accurate.

How they manage to do it is certainly one of the tricks of the trade; one more diplomatic secret that the general public is not privy to. Perhaps it is body language, lack of confidence or show of overconfidence; whatever they happen to be, they know how to do their job and do it so well that it is absolutely necessary for people appearing before them to make sure they have everything they need, rehearse their answers many times and don't make the mistake of assuming that their application will be approved simply because they think they have done everything right.

Again, the reputation of foreign consular officers for fairness and objectivity not only discourages any attempt on the part of the natives to try to influence them, but reinforces the belief that the best way to handle a visa application is to make every effort to do the right thing or when desperate enough, go through middlemen who seem to have figured out a way to do the impossible task of securing visas for those who have been denied.

This is another mystery. How do they do it? Do the middlemen actually succeed in obtaining visas for people? This will be discussed in another chapter.

CHAPTER ELEVEN

Problems and challenges to people traveling or immigrating to foreign countries

The most important aspect of the entire process is how to prepare to get the visa that would authorize you to travel to the country of your choice. We are repeating what has already been pointed out elsewhere because it is the most important phase of the process. And that is usually the most difficult as well as the most stressful part simply because most people from Third World countries in Africa and elsewhere know even before submitting an application that they might not get the visa they apply for. They know they are likely to be denied, especially if it is the first time they apply for a visa, in spite of the fact they have made every effort to comply with all the rules and regulations. We've discussed the reasons in another chapter.

Essentially, the assumption is that Third World applicants almost always fail to meet the requirements, whatever that means. That is the rationale and reason for the denial of the majority of visa applications from Africans and others from developing countries who seek visas from foreign embassies. The denials are supposedly caused by the inability of the applicants to meet the requirements. It's supposed to be that simple.

But check this out. The most common issues involved in traveling overseas and the immigration and emigration process usually tend to relate to what makes people decide to travel overseas or immigrate in the first place, why they chose certain countries, as opposed to others, what they do when they get there, what happens to them, the impact it has on their families, their religion, their native cultures, customs, and traditions. While these are perfectly legit and relevant issues, our focus at this point is on the most important aspect of the process: how to prepare to get the visa. The others will be discussed later.

IS IT POSSIBLE TO PREPARE IN A WAY THAT IMPROVES ONE'S CHANCES OF GETTING A VISA?

Again, the question becomes: is it possible to prepare in a way that can improve one's chances of getting a visa? And the answer is, yes. Indeed, a big yes. It is entirely and totally possible. It's like everything else. There is a way to go about it that can minimize and possibly eliminate the problems that can potentially contribute to your application's failure to meet the requirements

One thing is for sure, traveling or immigrating overseas to countries such as the United States, Canada, England, and Germany continues to be immensely attractive to the majority of the people in Africa, Asia, South America, and the Caribbean. No matter how hard it is to get the visa, the numbers of people seeking entry permits to foreign countries continue to increase. The United States, is by far the leading country of choice for the majority of visa applicants from around the world.

So what factors contribute to the decision to travel overseas or immigrate to certain foreign countries and not others? Do people know what to expect when they immigrate to another country? Does anyone plan to be an illegal immigrant?

WHY PEOPLE TRAVEL OVERSEAS WHEN THEY KNOW THEY WILL ENCOUNTER PROBLEMS GETTING THE IMMIGRANT VISA OR STAYING THERE

These questions and the others above have been probed, analyzed and examined by experts and writers over the years, in an attempt to understand why people decide to leave the countries in which they were born to travel to and live in a foreign country when they know they would confront problems. They are even aware that the problems they would face have the potential to change their lives, including the possibility of becoming an illegal immigrant when they are not able to change their visa status from non-immigrant to immigrant.

A variety of reasons have been offered over the years purporting to explain the reasons why people leave their native countries to travel to foreign countries and the immigration phenomenon. It has been suggested that immigration is seen by many as an alternative to a lifestyle that has ceased to offer any more challenges, and for which a change of environment is seen as a solution.

By far the most popular, and perhaps the most plausible explanation offered by experts is one which suggests that most immigrants leave their native countries in search of a better life elsewhere. They have made the decision that they stand a better chance of pursuing higher education, getting a better paying job, gaining access to better housing in another country. These are referred to as economically motivated immigrants.

The other group consists of political refugees. They leave their countries simply because they have no other choice, but flee for their lives. And no one can blame them. The right thing to do if your life is in danger in your own country is to find a safe place elsewhere.

What about those who have good jobs, or access to wealth in their native countries, yet travel overseas or immigrate?

While the notion of a search for a better life has some validity, it does not explain the reason why many immigrants who have the means to continue to live comfortable lives in their native countries or whose lives are not imperiled in any way also immigrate. The debate on that issue continues.

STORIES OF TRAGIC DEATHS OF IMMIGRANTS AND HORROR STORIES OF RAPE, TORTURE, AND MUTILATION OF TRAVELERS AND IMMIGRANTS ARE NOT MERE MEDIA HYPE. THEY ARE TRUE AND REAL

No matter how intense the media hype about the dangers involved in trying to cross borders without the proper papers, in spite of the drastic measures taken by governments to try to prevent both legal and illegal immigration, the flow of immigrants from country to country and continent to continent continues in a steady stream. And many come from developing countries in Africa and other parts of the Third World.

The desperation of people from Third World countries to travel and or immigrate to foreign countries has been well documented. Most people will do everything in their power to travel or immigrate overseas. Regardless of how long the journey takes, or the hazards and obstacles to be faced, and quite often the exorbitant fees charged by unscrupulous smugglers and criminals who become involved when those desperate to travel or immigrate seek their services, they manage to find the means, the willpower and the energy to do it.

Why they subject themselves to such dangers in order to travel or immigrate overseas is easy to understand: they have made up their minds that they stand a better chance of succeeding in a country other than their own. And once the decision is made to leave their native countries, they stick with it. Armed with such convictions, they head towards countries in Europe or the United States or Australia with the assumption that those countries offer them a better chance to get a job, gain an education or pursue a career, at least, they believe they can do much better in comparison to what they can do in their native countries. Or so it seems to those who don't know what the real deal is. And quite often, that is precisely the case; they have no idea what to expect in the countries to which they are traveling or immigrating.

With little or no knowledge about the politics, the racial climate, the economic conditions, the social and cultural conditions in the countries to which they are immigrating, they arrive to find out that they don't fit in, cannot speak the language, can't find jobs and are not welcomed or embraced by the native citizens. In the meantime, they have created another problem that makes it almost impossible for them to turn around and go back to their native countries. They might have sold everything they had, given up good jobs, or borrowed heavily to finance the trip. Returning home in the same condition in which they left isn't an option for most immigrants. They have to figure out a way to survive, find jobs and save money before they can go back home.

Others immigrate simply because they have no choice. They may be fleeing political persecution and oppression. For still others, traveling or immigrating to an overseas country may be the only way to avoid being killed. Many immigrants from the Middle East and a number of African countries had no choice but to leave or face death.

The point we are making here is that regardless of the motive for traveling or immigrating, there is the right way to go about it as well as the wrong way.

IT'S ABSOLUTELY NECESSARY YOU KNOW ABOUT THE FOREIGN COUNTRY YOU'RE TRAVELING OR IMMIGRATING TO

Once again, we want to emphasize that the last thing you want to do is to go to a foreign country about which you know little or nothing and expect to succeed in accomplishing your mission, whatever it may be. It won't happen, certainly not when you have no idea about the basic travel related actions required such as the documents that have to be filed to get an extension of your visa if the need arises for you to do so

It is impossible to know everything about a country in advance, but the least you can do is to know a few basic facts relating to such things as the culture, the politics, the basic economic, financial and social systems, the weather in the foreign country to which you are traveling, the kind of attire you will need to travel with at the time you are scheduled to leave your native country, and most importantly, the kind of entry visa you need to have and whether that visa will allow you to stay long enough to take care of the business that is taking you there. As improbable as it may seem, many people from Third World countries board planes for Europe and America and other places and have no idea what kind of visa they have, as fundamental and important as that information may be. All they know is they have a visa to go to another country. As far as they are concerned, that's all they need. Nothing else matters.

That's not good enough. You want to make sure before you leave that you have the right visa, and by the right visa, we mean the kind of entry visa that makes it possible for you to enter the country legally and stay long enough to accomplish the objectives you have in mind.

Timing is crucial. It is common for people from Third World countries to plan to travel to Europe and America or Canada in the middle of winter, a kind of weather they know nothing about and for which they may not be prepared. They have no idea about how to cope with the weather conditions in that part of the world. Consequently, they land at airports in the middle of winter in America and Europe when it is freezing cold with tropical clothing.

For a prospective immigrant, visitor, or tourist to any overseas country, the proper thing to do is to plan to travel and arrive at a time when the weather might be similar to or close to what exists in your country. Or find out about the weather and get the appropriate clothing. Here again, all that information and data are available on the Internet.

These are some of the things your travel agent will not tell you. They will assume you are already aware of these things when that may not be true. Plus, they don't really care about too much else besides getting paid for whatever services they might have rendered. Whether you survive, succeed, or fail overseas is entirely up to you.

CHAPTER TWELVE

Coping with the challenges and problems of living and working in a foreign country

Many people from Africa and Third World countries begin making mistakes the moment they arrive in foreign countries. They simply decide not to do anything about their status after they have managed to enter a foreign country on whatever visa they were given. With their minds made up to not return like they are supposed to, they make no effort to get a visa extension when their entry visas are about to expire. They even refuse to find out what options they might have to extend their visas in foreign countries, resigning themselves to the fact that there is nothing they can do about it. Just gaining entry to an overseas country is good enough for them. Nothing else matters.

THE WRONG WAY TO TRAVEL OR IMMIGRATE OVERSEAS IS TO HAVE THE MINDSET IN THE BEGINNING THAT ALL YOU HAVE TO DO IS TO FIND A WAY TO ENTER AN OVERSEAS COUNTRY

That is definitely the wrong approach by anyone who travels or immigrates to a foreign country, regardless of how long you plan to stay and for what reason. It doesn't really matter from which part of the world you come from, the color of your skin, or how much money you have. It is part of the process of making it possible for people to travel to live and do business or visit any country in the world. For those who know, it is only the beginning of a long and rather complicated process that will make it possible for you to stay for long as you want to, allow you to find a job, if you need one, or decide that's what you would like to do, or find housing. In brief, taking such an action will make you legal, give you certain rights and benefits and enable you to do the things everyone with the proper and legal status does.

MOST PEOPLE BECOME ILLEGAL ALIENS IN FOREIGN COUNTRIES AS A RESULT OF NOT DOING ANYTHING ABOUT CHANGING THEIR STATUS AND NOT KNOWING WHAT TO DO OR BEING AFRAID OF BECOMING INVOLVED IN THE SYSTEM

So why do people refuse to take the necessary actions required to avoid becoming an illegal alien when they arrive in a foreign country?

The reason why most people refuse to take further action after they arrive in overseas countries is easy to explain. They feel intimidated by a system they know little or nothing about. And that is enough to stop them from taking any action that would bring them to the attention of the authorities.

It's that simple. They don't want to get involved in a process that could potentially go wrong or give the authorities reason to ask more questions. They'd rather not get involved. Usually, this kind of approach creates more problems. They end up as illegal immigrants and get them in more trouble as a result. What they don't know is that there are options they may have just by virtue of being in the country legally at the time.

WHY YOU SHOULD NOT BE AFRAID OR FEEL INTIMIDATED

It has been argued that the majority of Africans that travel and immigrate to America and other foreign countries do so legally, to begin with. That assertion is essentially true. There is no way anyone will be able to board a plane in Accra, Ghana, Lagos, Nigeria or Cairo, Egypt with a ticket to America, Canada or Australia without some kind of a visa that would authorize entry. It's practically impossible.

Yet the same people who have arrived legally would end up as illegal aliens in part because they refuse to take further actions to extend their visa after they land, simply because they are afraid of what might happen if they get involved in a system that would keep track of them. Again, that is the wrong approach. Take action. Don't just sit back and do nothing. That's the worst possible mistake anyone can make.

There is no need to be afraid.

So what exactly is the action to take that many people seem to be afraid to take or just don't know about?

GETTING A VISA EXTENSION OR PROLONGING YOUR STAY IN AN OVERSEAS COUNTRY IS AN OPTION ALL TRAVELERS HAVE. EXERCISE THAT RIGHT.

It is called a visa extension or something similar in most countries around the globe. And it means precisely what it says: extending the visa that allowed you to enter the country. This is how it works. Anyone who travels to any overseas country as a non- immigrant, for a certain specified period, the initial visa given specifies how long you are supposed to stay.

What they don't tell you is what you can do when you decide to stay for a longer period; at least, they won't volunteer that information, if no one asks for it. And more than likely, most people won't ask for that kind of information. They don't want to ask any questions that would raise suspicions about them and possibly create problems with entering the country. At this point, they just want to enter that overseas country. They have not come that far and spent all that money to get stopped at the airport for asking stupid questions. As for the 'connection' people, they are even more unwilling to reveal that information or encourage you to pursue that option, fearing the possibility of more problems that could lead to them.

The truth is; that option is open to everyone who travels to any overseas country. Once you have gained access to any country, for any length of time, that option is open to you. Simply go ahead and ask for an extension of your stay if you decide that you need more time to finish your business.

NOT TAKING ANY ACTION ALWAYS LEADS TO BEING ILLEGAL

But the important thing to note is this: that option is open only to those who have a legal right to be in that country. In other words, you have to be in possession of a passport with a visa that allows you to enter that country, and most importantly, the visa has to be current when you apply for an extension. You cannot wait for the visa to expire before applying for an extension.

Again, the suggestion is to begin the process immediately, soon after arriving in the foreign country of your choice. It's the best time. You have some time on your visa at this point, and all you have to do is to ask for an extension based on the fact that you have not finished the business you wanted to take care of.

Offices of immigration authorities are easy to find in any part of the world, especially in the age of the Internet in which everything can be 'googled'

CHAPTER THIRTEEN

Surviving and succeeding in America, Europe, Australia, Canada and other foreign countries

Over the years, overseas countries have had an immense attraction for people from Third World countries. America, in particular, has emerged as one country that appears to present everyone with the opportunity to succeed, improve one's condition in life, at least, that is what one is led to believe. It is projected as a country where everyone can get a job that pays decent wages which in turn makes it possible to live a reasonably decent lifestyle.

But is America really the land of opportunity it is presumed to be? Does it present every immigrant with a level playing field? Are immigrants from the Third World as successful as other immigrants from other parts of the world in America when it comes to achieving the American Dream? What about countries in Europe with regard to respecting human rights pertaining to immigrants? Are Africans safe in Europe as they would be in America or vice versa? These are some of the fundamental issues that most immigrants have to contend with in one form or another.

MAJORITY OF IMMIGRANTS AND PEOPLE WHO GO OVERSEAS BEGIN LEGALLY WITH A VISA

Most immigrants, however, tend to be highly motivated, mostly driven by the need to not only survive but to be successful at whatever they do. Immigrants, from the Third World, in particular, view immigration as a means to an end. Thus they immigrate with one aim: to do whatever it takes in order to improve their lot in life. It is for this reason that many people from the Third World travel or immigrate to America, Europe, Asia and other places around the world.

On a daily basis, immigrants from Third World countries arrive in America and other foreign countries and begin the process of integrating into the community in which they settle. Some arrive as couples with children, but mostly, newly arrived immigrants tend to be single, preferring to test the waters first, settle down and then send for their spouses and kids, once they are secure. For the single men and women who have no spouses back home, the inevitable happens – they begin to socialize with non- immigrants, seeking to become involved in relationships that often end in marriages. For the most part, they live in communities with an ethnic mix of people from different nationalities.

Those with specialized training such as doctors and engineers seek and often find employment in their respective fields, and make good money as a result of the skills they bring to the job and the specialized nature of their qualifications.

GLOBAL VILLAGE MAKES IT POSSIBLE TO FEEL AT HOME FOR THIRD WORLD PEOPLE IN FOREIGN COUNTRIES.

The immigrant, as a student, a worker in a factory or as a professional, lives in a community of people with whom he or she interacts daily. Many immigrants are single and live alone. Others live with their families. Often, a few share apartments in groups of two or more.

Integrating into the general society offers considerable challenges to immigrants from the Third World. In the process, many are forced to abandon habits they have nurtured over the years, or adjust their behavioral patterns in order to be able to fit into a particular society. Most succeed; some encounter problems, others fail miserably. Question becomes: why do some succeed and others fail?

We come back to the same old question: how people from Third World countries prepare adequately to deal with the overseas life. Regardless of how long or short the stay and the reason for traveling overseas, you'll have to learn quickly how to behave in such a way that your neighbors and all others with whom you interact will not feel compelled to distance themselves from you for one reason or another. And it's not a very difficult thing to do if you know what is involved.

CHAPTER FOURTEEN

Where to find the right information
about overseas countries

The primary sources of information for the majority of people in the Third World about traveling and living overseas are immigrants who return home temporarily or permanently from Europe and America and other parts of the world. Information gained from such immigrants who have returned home to their villages, towns and cities would seem to be the easiest and the most convenient way for people to learn about life overseas. Well, it is not. Quite often, it is the most misleading. The returning immigrants don't always tell the real story.

Airports around the world are filled everyday with immigrants and non- immigrants living and working in foreign countries flying to different cities in Third World countries. They are returning to their native countries. The majority usually travel with round-trip tickets, suggesting they would return to wherever they came from. Others may have one way tickets; they are not going back. Many may be legal residents or naturalized citizens, able to leave and enter the country to which they have immigrated at will, while those with one-way tickets will not go back because they cannot or have decided not to, or will not be allowed to return because they don't have the correct 'papers'. Quite a few may be students who have finished their courses of study, or they are immigrants who have completed the seasonal migratory work and are heading home to wait for the next season.

Some may be leaving under duress, forced out by an order of deportation or they may be absconding from the law. They majority are doing what is expected of them: going back home to reconnect with family and friends they left behind.

Also, the death of an important member of the family back home is another significant reason to take a trip home for most immigrants from Third World countries. For many African tribes, the death of an important member of the family back home, such as a parent or an uncle, is viewed as a serious enough event to warrant a trip back home, no matter where you are. In some tribes and families, it is imperative that all members of the family be present for certain rites to be performed. Those absent, for whatever reason, and therefore unable to participate in the ritual may miss out on the benefits bestowed on those who take part. What the advantages and disadvantages are cannot be easily explained.

Others take trips back home so they can monitor projects they have undertaken, such as a house under construction or a business started or simply to show off that they have some hard earned Euros, dollars or francs to spend.

PEOPLE FROM THIRD WORLD COUNTRIES WHO LIVE IN AMERICA AND EUROPE AND RETURN HOME ARE NOT THE BEST SOURCES OF INFORMATION ON LIFE OVERSEAS

Presumed to be first-hand information from those who have been exposed to it in real life, people back home ask relatives, friends, and townsfolk who live overseas to tell them about the kind of life they live abroad. The problem is that the returning immigrants don't always tell the real story. If most immigrants are to be believed, life overseas makes it possible to make lots of money. They tell tall tales of the new life in the foreign country to which they have immigrated, about the new cars they drive, the beautiful houses they live in, and big money in their bank accounts. They make it seem as though they live a good life.

WHY PEOPLE FROM THIRD WORLD COUNTRIES WHO RETURN HOME DON'T TELL THE TRUTH ABOUT LIFE OVERSEAS.

The problem with these kinds of stories is they're not always true. There is a tendency to embellish them so the image of the immigrant will be enhanced in the eyes of the people back home. They want to be seen as successful. Only on rare occasions do immigrants tell the real story.

But in the process of making themselves look good in the eyes of their people back home, returning immigrants from Third World countries create a problem. They reinforce the perception that going overseas is the answer to all problems. And that is not the case. The truth sometimes is that back in the U. S. or England or wherever the immigrant lives, he or she may have a job that pays the minimum wage, or less in many instances, especially for those who are illegal or have no 'papers'. They manage to survive and save just about enough to make it possible to take a trip back home when it becomes absolutely necessary with enough Euros, francs and dollars to spend and 'live large', but ready and able to fly back out when the foreign currency runs out in part because they have return tickets..

WHY YOU SHOULDN'T BELIEVE WHAT AMERICANS AND EUROPEANS TELL YOU ABOUT THEIR COUNTRIES: THEY MAY NOT KNOW WHAT IS INVOLVED IN THE IMMIGRANT LIFE IN THEIR COUNTRY

Another source of misinformation are Europeans, Americans, Canadians, Australians, and others from developed countries in business, academia, government service, tourists, students, and others who find one reason or another to visit or reside in other countries. While overseas, they come into contact with the indigenous people in many different ways and at different levels and often serve as sources of information for those seeking to know about life overseas. Quite often, they have no real knowledge or information to give.

The recurring theme in these discussions is the fact that most people in Third World countries are misinformed about the immigrant life overseas. They have little or no idea of what it is all about. We also hold the view that a great number of immigrants from many parts of the Third World would have stayed home if they had access to accurate information concerning life for the immigrant in many of the countries in Europe, North America and elsewhere. In other words, if they know before they leave their countries of origin that they may run into problems overseas, become illegal aliens, be treated like second class citizens and criminals, be deported for not having 'papers', among other things they would look at other options besides traveling or immigrating overseas..

It is also evident that the majority of immigrants from developing countries don't know what to expect in a foreign country in terms of the problems they might have to face, or the changes they have to go through as immigrants. Many have no idea that as an immigrant, their status in most countries is no different from that of second-class citizens or in some cases, that they are treated like criminals. They don't know that there is a lot of bureaucratic red tape to go through in order to continue to reside legally in the country of choice, that deportation and other forms of harassment are often used to control the movement of immigrants.

IMMIGRANTS AND TRAVELERS TO FOREIGN COUNTRIES OFTEN TREATED LIKE CRIMINALS OR SECOND AND THIRD CLASS CITIZENS

It has been argued that if those who had already experienced the immigrant life overseas and had returned home to visit or retire simply tell the truth about the realities of the immigrant life overseas, especially for immigrants from Third World countries, there is the likelihood that a lot of people would either change their minds about immigrating or traveling to a foreign country and stay right where they are, or make sure they are fully prepared to deal with the challenges and problems that inhere in living in a foreign country. They would know what life for an immigrant overseas is all about, and will be aware whether they are prepared to deal with it or have the temperament and the guts to go through with it.

But that is not the case. Third World immigrants who return home seem to be unable to resist the temptation to be less than truthful about the kind of jobs they have and the money they make overseas. The lies and misrepresentations make them look good, making them appear to be doing well overseas and quite often, they have the funds to spend when they go back home to visit.

Not surprisingly, it creates huge problems for many immigrants from Third World countries after they have immigrated to countries in North America, Europe, etc when they find out that what they had been told is not true. Some end up as illegal immigrants, becoming part of a problem faced by most countries around the world with large populations of immigrants who went about it the wrong way.

CHAPTER FIFTEEN

Secrets your travel agent, middleman or 'connection' man or woman won't tell you

Do the 'connection' or middlemen actually succeed in obtaining the right visas for people? If so, how are they able to do it?

It all depends on the kind of visa the applicant seeks. Operated as an underground and clandestine network in countries like Ghana, Nigeria and other Third World countries, the 'connections' operation is not easy to penetrate and the inner workings of the syndicate are not known to most people. Also those who deal with them usually have no reason to go public with anything, fearing reprisals they might not be prepared for. Another thing works in their favor. The majority of their clients leave their native countries anyway, after they get their visas and are only too glad to have been able to get any kind of visa that makes it possible for them to board a plane and fly out. At that point, they are not interested in anything else, including the fact that they might have been given the wrong or a fake visa. All they want to do is to get out, and the sooner and the quieter the better. That's how desperate and naïve some people can be, making them easy targets for criminals to exploit.

WHY PEOPLE GO TO MIDDLEMEN AND 'CONNECTION' PEOPLE TO HELP THEM GET VISAS

Again, the methods used to obtain a visa do not necessarily interest the visa recipients. All they are interested in is to get a visa that would enable them to get out of the country. The only time middlemen have to be concerned is when things go wrong, that is, when a visa holder is refused entry to a foreign country for which he or she had been issued an entry permit. It at this point that the question comes to the fore: What kind of visas do middlemen get their clients?

It might be too late then to do anything about it. The victim might be in detention somewhere in a foreign country or sent back home.

This is the question most people who enlist the services of middlemen or any other source are supposed to ask before they agree to pay the fees charged. What kind of visa? Usually, they don't ask any questions because they don't want to stop anything in progress, but mostly because they have made up their minds that they don't really care about what's going on. All they are interested in and want to know is that arrangements will be made to get a visa that will get them into a foreign country.

WHY PEOPLE WHO GET VISAS FROM 'CONNECTION' PEOPLE USUALLY END UP AS ILLEGAL ALIENS AND STRANDED IN FOREIGN COUNTRIES

Therein lies the problem, not for the middlemen, but for the prospective immigrant. Rarely are the middlemen able to get immigrant visas. The process for that particular kind of visa is too involved and complicated. They usually succeed in securing visitor's visas for their clients, but don't take the time or the trouble to explain the true nature of the visa to them. They don't tell their clients that with a visitor's visa, they only have a limited number of days in which their visit to that particular country for which they have been issued a visa is valid.

HOW PEOPLE BECOME VICTIMS IN THEIR SEARCH FOR HELP TO GET A VISA TO A FOREIGN COUNTRY.

The middlemen know their clients are desperate and are driven only by the desire to leave the country. Level of education or awareness of world affairs plays little or no role here. Victims have included men and women with university degrees as well as those with no education. All of them fall prey to middlemen who manage to convince them to pay huge amounts for visas that are only valid for a short time or fake.

It can be assumed that knowing the true details of the visa situation probably wouldn't matter much to prospective immigrants anyway, even if they knew the truth. They will still make the attempt to leave, hoping that once they enter the country for which they had been issued a visa, they can convert from a visitor's status to that of a permanent immigrant.

What the victims don't know is that with a visitor's visa

in a country such as the United States, it is almost impossible to change from one status to another, that it is illegal to look for a job; or to get a social security number that allows one to seek employment. You cannot do anything except try to avoid the police and immigration authorities so you don't get caught, put in jail or deported to your native country.

CHAPTER SIXTEEN

Why people choose certain overseas countries to travel or immigrate to and avoid others

A familiar sight at United States embassies around the world continues to be large numbers of native citizens who gather there early in the morning, waiting to be called to be interviewed about their applications for visas to America. Their mission is to do whatever it takes to get the chance to plead their case to be considered for a visa to travel or immigrate to the United States. Many travel long distances to get to consular offices in faraway capital cities, and seem not to mind the tedium of waiting for hours, just to be interviewed by an embassy official. They are determined to get a visa to America and would do whatever it takes to make it happen.

WAYS OF APPLYING FOR VISA TO AMERICA, EUROPE AND ELSEWHERE HAVE CHANGED, FOR THE BETTER

The interview session between the applicant for a visa and an embassy official does not take too long, if everything is in order. If all the necessary documents are produced, and the correct answers are given to the satisfaction of the embassy official, it can be concluded in a matter of minutes.

One of the reasons is because the system of applying for a visa has been modernized and streamlined as a result of modern technology. It's done mostly online these days. Applicants are advised to go online to make an appointment and submit information that will give them a fairly good idea about who you are, what your intentions are, your 'binding ties' to your native country, and how to deal with your application. The system is so effective that embassy and consular officials basically know everything they need to know before you get there for the interview. They are as prepared for you as you may be and will base their decision on the answers you give to the questions they ask, in addition to the answers already provided on the forms you have submitted.

This is the moment many dread and yet look forward to; the few minutes before an embassy official which can either open the door to a new world or slam it shut and dash any hopes they had of leaving their native country.

There's no magic formula to it. Let no one fool you into thinking that you can outsmart or lie your way into a visa to a country like America. It's all about doing your homework, as we have already pointed out.

AMERICA IS STILL THE COUNTRY OF CHOICE FOR MOST PEOPLE WHO WANT TO TRAVEL OR IMMIGRATE TO AN OVERSEAS COUNTRY.

The media have described the scenes at U.S. embassies in different countries around the globe as very busy, often showing teeming crowds of natives seeking all kinds of visas.

They arrive early, ready to wait, no matter how long it takes for their turn to be called for the interview.

When the embassy office opens for business, usually only a few get called. The rest have to return the next day to repeat the process until their turn comes to be interviewed. Other foreign embassies draw crowds seeking visas, but American embassies around the globe almost always have the largest concentration of prospective immigrants and non- immigrants trying to get visas to travel to America, more evidence of the immense attraction that the United States has for people all over the world.

IS AMERICA SAFE FOR AFRICANS AND OTHERS FROM THIRD WORLD COUNTRIES?

If the media is to be believed, the United States is not the safest place to travel or immigrate to, if you happen to be a native of any African or any other Third World country. They report incidents in which people of African heritage appear to be more likely to be put in harm's way than others. There is supposed to be more violence and crime in neighborhoods in which people of African heritage live. It has also been argued that you may be denied a certain kind of job, housing, educational opportunities based on the fact that you come from a certain part of the world and have a certain pigmentation.

The question becomes: is it mere hype or real?

Many people from Third World countries who have lived in America have different things to say when it comes to their interpretation of the reality of life for people of African heritage. Some would agree that they don't feel safe simply as a result of being Africans and West Indians in America and the possibility of being victimized for being who they are or living in a certain neighborhood. At this point it becomes part of the larger question of race and equality and all the other factors involved. And that is not what we are here for. We'll leave that alone for the media analysts and pundits.

CHAPTER SEVENTEEN

How to prepare to immigrate or travel to another country with a different culture

Integrating into the general society in foreign countries offers considerable challenges to people from Third World countries that travel or immigrate overseas. In the process of mainstreaming, many are forced to abandon habits, norms and traditions they were raised with and have nurtured over the years and adjust their lifestyle in order to be able to fit into a particular society. Most succeed; some encounter problems, others fail miserably. Like everything else, there are success stories and abysmal failures. It's all about knowing what to expect and how to deal with the problems and challenges they face.

Generally, immigrants from the Third World tend to succeed in overcoming the challenges and pitfalls they face in making the transition from life in their native countries to life in the new environment. To many, it is not a big deal; at least, they don't make it seem like anything they can't deal with They figure out a way to make the necessary adjustments and adaptations and life goes on.

Others grope their way along, overwhelmed by almost everything they come across, unable to make the transition, stuck in their old ways, full of regrets for making the decision to travel or immigrate, but not quite ready to go back home.

By the same token, all of them appear to succumb to some of the pressures and problems that exist in the new environment into which they have settled. For instance, some of the more serious psycho-social problems like depression, stress, nervous breakdowns, and suicides that are quite common in most foreign countries, are not as common in Third World cultures. The majority of Third World cultures don't even recognize these as real diseases to worry about or that have to be clinically treated. But as immigrants in America, Canada, Europe, Australia, and other foreign countries, Third World immigrants tend to become vulnerable to various psycho-social problems including those mentioned above.

Why? It has been suggested that it is caused by trying too hard to change their native lifestyles as part of the process of making the transition from life over there in their native countries to life over where they happen to be in foreign countries. True or not is hard to say. Yet questions continue to be asked that reflect the concern of those who want to know what's going on. Not surprisingly, no one appears to know the real answers.

Some of the questions that have been asked include the following: can Third World people who are planning to travel or immigrate to countries like America, Germany, and Canada better prepare themselves to deal with the problems they are likely to face?

Does culture have an impact on Third World immigrants as they deal with problems and challenges in America, Europe, etc.? What are some of the potential problems an immigrant is likely to have to deal with, and how can people from Third

World countries deal with them successfully? What does one have to do in order to prevent them from running into serious problems? Why are some successful in foreign countries in finding jobs, or doing business and others are not able to do the same?

There are no easy answers to the above questions. But one thing is certain. There are common areas that pose a challenge and have the potential to become problematic to every immigrant or traveler from another country when it comes to living and working in a country that is different from what they have been used to in their native country culturally, socially, economically and politically. The challenges and problems that they have to contend with include but are not limited to the following:

Language: Anyone from an English speaking country who travels to France, Belgium or Germany is making a big mistake unless they happen to be proficient in the official languages of those countries. It just doesn't make sense to go to a country whose language you can't speak, but again, that doesn't stop many from doing just that. That might be their only chance of getting out of their country. Here is our advice. It's best to make every effort to go to a country where you won't have a problem communicating with the people, unless of course, you absolutely have no choice. That way, you eliminate a major problem.

Religion: When they are able to live in close proximity to each other, or have sufficient numbers in any city to create any kind of ethnic, social or cultural presence, immigrants from Third World countries make their presence known and felt in many ways, particularly in religion, and recreation. Those who identify themselves as Christians go to regular churches like the

Catholic, Baptist, Anglican, and Presbyterian churches where they join others in worship. Those who identify themselves as Muslims also join others of the same faith to worship in mosques alongside other immigrants from different parts of the world.

For others, religious worship is given an ethnic and cultural flavor when enough numbers congregate that share a common language and culture and are able to conduct their religious ceremonies in a native language. This is most evident in huge metropolitan areas like New York, Washington, Chicago, London, Paris, and Berlin and others too many to mention here. Religion, therefore, plays an important role in the immigrant community, especially when it comes to such occasions as weddings, funeral and memorial services.

Race: The globalized nature of the population mix around the world is quite visible in most cities around the world. No matter where you happen to be in America or Europe, more than likely, you'll see the ethnic mix when you walk the streets. There are the white Caucasians, Africans, Black Americans, Asians, Indians, Chinese, Hispanics or Latinos. And a whole lot of other people who belong to various ethnicities.

In its most simple and basic form, all societies consist of a diverse mixture of all races, with "race" meaning a group of people who share similar physical characteristics, cultural traditions, and social institutions. But race breaks down further into ethnicities, and in places such as Europe and America, ethnicity plays a significant role in the social structure. Which means you will stand out and be noticed for who you are: You will be noticed as a Third World person if that's what you happen to be. As a result, others will react to you in ways that reflect what they think about Third World people or whatever else you happen to be.

How do you deal with such a situation?

Go with the flow, will be the best advice. In other words, don't try to resist the need to conform by doing something that can bring attention to you. Just enjoy the life and people and culture around you and you won't have anything to worry about. Most importantly, you can continue to practice whatever lifestyle and culture you chose, so long as it doesn't break any rules or regulations.

Social and Economic Background:

Ethnic communities in American cities form as a result of the great numbers of people who share a common ethnic heritage and who live in close proximity, to each other whether as recent immigrants or as naturalized citizens of the countries to which they have immigrated. For the most part, immigrants from most of the Third World (Africa, South and Central America, the Caribbean) follow the same pattern as they integrate into cities and communities in America and Europe. There are sizeable communities that are characterized as Hispanic or Latino and may be dominated by people from Puerto Rico, Cuba, and the Dominican Republic, El Salvador, etc, etc. The link between them is forged basically by the common language they all speak. Spanish speaking immigrants from other parts of the Third World and immigrants from other countries such as Haiti and Jamaica have been able to emerge as distinct ethnic blocks in certain areas in cities around the world. And the defining characteristics are pretty much the same: businesses run by people from the same country, providing services and meeting the needs of members of their community, in addition to enough numbers living close to each other and so on and so forth.

WHY AFRICANS ARE NOT ALWAYS ABLE TO EMERGE AS DISTINCT GROUPS WITH A STRONG AND NOTICEABLE NEIGHBORHOOD PRESENCE IN AMERICA AND EUROPE

Immigrants from Africa, on the other hand, have not been able to form ethnic blocks as others have done for a number of reasons, not the least of which is the fact that the numbers are not there. Africans do not, are not able to travel and immigrate to America and Europe and elsewhere in sufficient enough numbers for reasons already stated. The difficulty in getting the visa is one of the primary reasons. Furthermore, until recently, immigrants from Africa do not usually live in close proximity to each other to be able to create an ethnic presence. Perhaps the most important reason why Africans are not able to emerge as a distinct immigrant group is because most do not make a concerted or conscious effort to protect, project and maintain their identities as Africans when they travel overseas. While it is relatively easy to identify a Jamaican because of the "dreads" and or the Caribbean accent, Africans for the most part tend to gravitate towards embracing the fashions and cultures in the countries they travel or immigrate to and may be identified only by their accents. The younger generation tends to be more ready and able to change and adapt. Again, this has changed somewhat lately.

Cultural:

In most immigrant communities, however, an attempt is made to keep alive many of the customs and traditions that the people knew and practiced back home. This is especially characteristic of first-generation immigrants and on such occasions as naming ceremonies when a newly born baby is introduced to other members of the community or at funerals, memorial services, and sometimes at weddings. Most of the ceremonies are performed in accordance with tribal customs and traditions, sometimes to the bemusement and fascination of non Africans who may be seeing such a ritual for the first time. And in most instances, most immigrants tend to define their cultural identity through the costumes they wear on such occasions.

Immigrants from the African community have emerged over the years as one of the more culture conscious immigrant groups, wherever they happen to be, whether in Europe, America or Australia, especially the females. They are known to wear their traditional costumes and fashions when they go to church, or on any special occasion which celebrates an important event, be it a death or a birth, or a national celebration. The kente cloth, now a popular fashion item in America and Europe started becoming popular when it was worn by Ghanaians in foreign countries. Everybody, especially African-Americans and West Indians loved it, tried it, and its popularity soared until it became so popular that it has been adopted as the virtual symbol for Afro-centric consciousness among African Americans and Africans alike, as well as others from the Caribbean.

Food

Most people from Third World countries don't care for or simply can't seem to develop an appetite for fast food, especially those popular in North America and Europe, no matter how hard they try. They prefer to eat home-cooked food, prepared by themselves or people they know, a habit which develops as a result of being born and raised in environments where cooking is part of the daily routine of life.

On the other hand, fast food and takeout food from restaurants tend to be the popular choices in many overseas countries, particularly the United States. As a result, food can become an issue for some people from Third World countries when they travel overseas and the question becomes: what to do about food?

Usually, three options present themselves in such a situation

1. Get into the habit of eating fast foods, or cooking cuisine common and popular in the country and culture in which they live. If they live in the United States, for instance, it will be the usual all American cuisine.

2. Make no attempt to accommodate eating habits and foods in the new environment. It means foreign cuisine and foreign food. And that is not too difficult to do these days. We'll explain in due course how that has been made possible with the emergence of ethnic and specialty grocery stores all over the world

3. Combine the two; mix eating habits and cuisine from the native country with those of the new environment and make the best of it. Preferred by many, this has resulted in the creation of a wide range of unique dishes and cooking and eating patterns in many parts of the world, most notably in Europe and North America.

FAST FOODS LEAST LIKED BY THIRD WORLD TRAVELERS AND IMMIGRANTS IN AMERICA AND EUROPE

The first option has little or no attraction for most people from different races, cultures, particularly those from Third

World countries. With tastes and palates firmly established from back home, they find it difficult to abandon their style of cooking, eating habits and cuisine in favor of American or European-style cooking and cuisine. The majority make the effort, in response to pressure and enticements from others, and sometimes succeed in making the transition as part of the process of mainstreaming. Others either just refuse to do so or are not able to and blame it on a number of factors which include such claims as the food is too bland, not spicy enough, too processed, etc.

To them, immigrating to another country does not mean changing one's eating habits. Their old eating habits are viewed as a part of their cultural identity. Any attempt to substitute the old with something new is seen as no less than a betrayal and a denial of one's heritage.

This is the type of individual who makes a conscious and concerted effort to keep old habits alive by continuing to practice them. They are not willing to make any compromises. Others from different races and cultures who deal with them are sometimes pressured or cajoled into learning how to cook foreign foods they do not particularly care for themselves.

HOW THIRD WORLD PEOPLE MANAGE TO HOLD ON TO THEIR CULTURES IN FOREIGN COUNTRIES

They are able to maintain their old eating habits in foreign countries mainly as a result of another aspect of the globalization of the international community, brought about partly by immigration and technology in most cities around the world. These are community-based ethnic stores that make it possible to obtain food ingredients from different parts of the world. They import food items that are distributed, marketed and promoted with immigrant communities in mind.

The specialty ethnic stores cater specifically to a market created as a result of the presence of immigrants in most metropolitan areas all over the world. In countries such as the United Kingdom, U. S., and Canada, ethnic grocery stores have become big business. They are in large cities as well as small towns, usually operated by immigrant families and stock all kinds of food items and specialty products.

ETHNIC STORES AND BUSINESSES IN OVERSEAS COUNTRIES PROVIDE WHAT THIRD WORLD IMMIGRANTS AND TRAVELERS NEED

They advertise and promote themselves in various ways; as import and export businesses in large metropolitan areas and sell other ethnic-based consumer products besides food items such as furniture, clothing, etc. In smaller cities, they adopt a more direct ethnic profile, by describing themselves as Oriental food stores, Korean stores, African food stores or Caribbean food stores, which makes it a lot easier for people to know where to go to get what they need.

Also in most cities in Europe and the United States, the majority of regular grocery stores create and maintain sections dedicated to foreign foods, giving people from other countries the choice to shop for food items that can be used to prepare a variety of foreign dishes.

The third option basically is an exercise in creative cooking. Here an attempt is made to blend the two worlds that have come together as a result of travel and immigration. They try to create something that is not too different from what they know. Most succeed in doing so, though it requires a considerable degree of culinary expertise.

Rice comes to mind as one food item that can be easily adapted. One of the most popular staple foods consumed by most people from different parts of the world, it is widely accepted that the way in which it is prepared is what makes it different. Flavored and cooked in a slightly different way, the end product usually comes out just about right enough to satisfy all cultural palates.

So are the different varieties of stews, soups, and breads as well as many other dishes. Here again, the specialty ethnic store plays a role in supplying some of the ingredients such as the spices, with the rest to be gotten from regular grocery stores. It's all in the cooking: the way it is done, how long it is cooked, and the spices used that contribute to making food taste, feel and look different, making it less of a problem or none at all, in situations where food becomes an issue as a result of traveling or immigrating from one country to another

Fashions: You'll have to forget about pride in ethnic identity for a while when you travel to another country unless you want to stick out like a sore thumb and bring a whole lot of attention to yourself.

To what degree do the above factors impact an individual when it comes to traveling or immigrating to another country?

It's not known in precise terms what impact or role they play in the process. One thing remains constant. They have to be dealt with in one way or another, and how the people involved handle them pretty much determines how successful they would be in their life overseas.

Why do some succeed and others fail? Is there a special way to handle such situations that enhances one's chances of traveling to and living successfully in an overseas country? How do other people handle similar situations?

Again, that's what this book is about: to discuss, analyze and find solutions to problems and challenges faced by those planning to or already involved in the process of trying to obtain a visa, also referred to as entry permit that would authorize them to leave their country for a destination in a foreign country.

CHAPTER EIGHTEEN

How To Settle In A Foreign Country: Best Tips

You could have a wide variety of reasons for traveling, moving or immigrating to an overseas country. A job, love, family or business can provide a sufficiently strong enough reason for anyone to seriously consider leaving their native country to travel overseas for a brief period or an extended stay. While the move itself could be quite easy, settling into unfamiliar settings could be harder than you know.

The popular assumption is that adapting to the culture of your new home and becoming a part of another country takes time and effort but is surely possible. While settling in a foreign country is by no means an easy task, it is doable and can become a life changing experience in more ways than one. It all depends on the individual involved, the degree to which he or she has prepared to deal with life in a new environment, the purpose for which they undertook the journey, and most importantly, the resources available to them. In other words, it is imperative that you plan well, get as much information as you possibly can about the country to which you are seeking a visa and take the necessary actions to prepare for life in a different country. So now the question becomes; what are some of the necessary steps one can take before traveling to an overseas country so you will hit the ground running, so to speak?

Learn The Language

It makes sense to make every effort to learn the language of the new land to which you have travelled or immigrated. At least, know enough of the lingua franca to be able to navigate your way around independently, using the language of the land that everybody uses.

Your day to day life becomes much easier and you are in a much better position when it comes to interacting and conversing with the locals. Again, learning the language of the new land is the easiest way to start settling in any foreign country. Knowing the language makes it much easier for you to move around, understand what is being said around you and help you settle in your new home.

For a lot of people, there is no need to learn a new language. They avoid the language problems altogether by goong to a counrry where there is no need for them to learn the language in order to be able to communicate and interact with the natives. They find a solution to the problem by going to a country where the lingua franca, local language, is familiar or known to them.. For instance, it makes perfect sense for someone who is familiar with the French laguage to chose to travel or immigrate to France to do business or seek medical attention or immigrate. The same applies for people who speak and write Engish to travel to England, Canada or America. It makes life a lot less difficult for all involved, especially, the traveler. Here again, you hit the ground running.

Be Adventurous and Curious about Your New Surroundings.

You have begun an adventure the moment you make the decision to travel or immigrate to a foreign country. It is an adventure that will continue for a long, long time that will involve dealing with people with different ideas on almost everything you know. The ideal thing to do is try to know what you are dealing with in terms of the basic and fundamental things that exist in that new environment. And you can do that by allowing yourself to be part of any activity or program that makes it possible to learn about the people and their ways. When your colleagues and acquaintances in the foreign country ask you to join in on some fun, don't shy away or come up with some kind of excuse as to why you can't join. Go with the flow. Let everything you do be part of the adventure. . Before you know, you will begin to like it and start having fun.

Take Up A Course Or Join A Group

There had to have been an activity that you enjoyed back home. Take it up again as soon as you can in your new country. You'll find people with similar interests and end up making new friends. Finding similarities in your new home can help you to integrate, mix and adapt to your new surroundings much faster.

Study The Culture

We have already pointed out in other chapters, the importance of seeking, finding and learning about the cultures and traditions of the foreign country you are traveling or immigrating to. Being totally ignorant about the basic and fundamental cultural practices can create big problems. Not only are you creating the impression that you could care less about their customs and traditions; you may be setting yourself up to do or say something that could offend certain cultural sensibilities or norms in part because you don't know, and not because you have no respect. That's how they will interpret your wrong actions, until you get the chance to explain things. Meanwhile, the damage is done as a result of your ignorance.

For instance, burping at the dinner table won't be considered offensive in some Third World countries while in most European nations it can be frowned upon.

The color red is bad luck in a country like Korea while it is considered as a lucky color in China. Understanding these nuances can go a long way in making the locals appreciate the efforts you take in trying to understand and appreciate their norms, traditions and ways of living.

Don't Be Afraid To Ask For Help

Don't ever be afraid of asking for help when you find yourself in a different country. You're in unfamiliar, unknown surroundings. It can be quite easy for you to get lost or even get into trouble with local laws that you might not know about.

When you need help, ask for it. The locals in most places will go out of their way to make you feel at home in their country. There is nothing more like feeling at home abroad than the acceptance of the locals.

Keep In Touch With Your Family And Friends

Moving to a new place can be quite overwhelming, especially if you don't know anyone or the language. The feeling of loneliness can be quite suffocating as well. You can counter the feeling of loneliness by making every effort to stay in touch with your friends back home. We live in a world of smart technology, smart phones and the Internet that make it possible to call, connect with and communicate with people in the farthest reaches of the globe. Use these technologies to the max. You'll feel much safer in your new home abroad if you stay in touch with the folks back home by using available technology.

While moving to a new country can be quite tough, being open-minded, friendly, and fun can open up a lot of doors for you which will help you settle in. These tips have been very helpful to others in similar situations. Hopefully, they will help you as much as they have helped others.

CHAPTER NINETEEN

Secrets to surviving and succeeding overseas: what you need to know before you get there

Let us begin with a very common scenario. Somehow you have succeeded in getting a visa in your native country that allowed you to travel or immigrate to a foreign country. You managed to find the means to buy a ticket, board a plane and have disembarked in a city in a strange new land. What do you do now?

You don't know anyone and you really don't have a lot of money. Can you simply say to yourself that you will be okay because you have succeeded in landing in a foreign country?

Believe it or not, it has happened in real life. Many have done just that. And many more will probably try to do it the same way, regardless of the fact that they know it's the wrong way to travel or immigrate to any overseas country. People from Third World countries usually fall under this category.

They are ready to risk it all. They will grab any chance that comes their way or simply push themselves to do whatever it takes to travel or immigrate to a foreign country. We have cited instances in which people allow themselves to be coerced into believing they can cross deserts on foot, sail across seas in boats that are not seaworthy and allow themselves to be locked inside trucks without ventilation that will travel long distances. They turn to such drastic ways of gaining access to foreign countries basically as a result of not having the proper visa and, quite often, the resources that would make it possible for them to travel or immigrate to a foreign country.

Then there are those who take the risk of traveling or immigrating to a foreign country with visas that authorize them to enter the overseas country only for a brief period after which they become illegal. To such people, the prospect of becoming illegal is not enough to discourage them from applying for or making arrangements to get visas that last for a short period or even ask for and get visas that are forged or fake. We have compiled a list that breaks down the reasons why it is the wrong thing to do to enter an overseas country illegally.

REASONS WHY YOU SHOULD NOT ENTER ANY OVERSEAS COUNTRY ILLEGALLY

Entering any overseas country illegally places you in a position where you are regarded as a criminal. In many countries around the world; such people are referred to as illegal aliens and that makes you a criminal, for all intents and purposes. A criminal is the last thing you want to be in a foreign country.

As an illegal alien in any foreign country, you will not be able to go out and look for a job because you may not be in possession of the document that gives you the right to work. In a country like the United States, a social security number is required whenever and wherever you do anything that calls for you to identify yourself, which includes applying for a job, renting an apartment, obtaining a driver's license, getting medical attention in a hospital. Just about every situation in which you interact with officialdom or the public calls for some kind of identification to verify who you are or who you claim to be. Everyone who is a legal resident has a social security number in America. Not having a social security number simply means you are illegal and not part of the system. Again, it is used for everything, including applying for a job, finding housing and other forms of accommodation, even applying to purchase a vehicle. Life without it is impossible in a country like America.

You may be denied medical attention in a hospital if you cannot produce a social security number or any other form of identification. In other words, you have to pray not to get sick if you don't have' papers' in a country like America. If you do get sick and report to a hospital without a social security number, you run the risk of someone from the hospital alerting the authorities about an illegal alien wanting to receive medical attention. You might be arrested in the waiting room and deported just for seeking medical care.

Without a social security number, you cannot enroll in any educational institution and will be denied the right to pursue higher education or benefit from the educational system in any shape or form

Worse yet, you cannot open and maintain a bank account or send money to anyone inside or outside the country by Western Union or Moneygram because your status as an illegal alien denies you that privilege.

You are on the 'wanted list' like a criminal until you change your status from illegal alien without a social security number to a legal permanent resident with a social security number. Any time you get involved in a situation in which law enforcement authorities are involved, there is the likelihood that you would be asked to show proof of your status. A social security number will do the trick if you don't have any other form of identification.

Not having a social security number has proven to be one of the leading ways that the authorities use to look for and find illegal aliens. Just driving down the street in a car with a broken taillight or failure to signal a turn can lead to the vehicle being stopped and everyone inside being ordered to show an ID. Many Third World illegal aliens have found themselves in trouble and deported this way.

It has been suggested elsewhere that the right thing to do is to begin the process of getting an ID immediately. No matter what it is, the fact remains that you entered the country legally, to begin with, and have some leeway to get some kind of consideration based on the fact that you are making an effort to comply with the law.

HAVE A SKILL. YOU ARE BETTER OFF IF YOU HAVE SOME KIND OF A SKILL

It has been suggested that one's chances of succeeding in Europe or America or elsewhere as an immigrant is enhanced greatly if you have some kind of a skill that you can use to get a job. No matter what skill you may have, it is better than not having any at all.

Most Third World people have no idea how people with skills are highly regarded in foreign countries. It's a lot easier for them to get hired. They make reasonably decent wages, using the skills they have acquired to help fix other people's problems. We suggest that you make every effort to have some kind of a skill as a carpenter, plumber, and auto mechanic, just to mention a few.

At the end of the day, people will do precisely what they want to do when it comes to finding a way to travel to or immigrate to an overseas country. They will do it by any means necessary, taking risks and getting themselves into situations that put their lives in danger. Once they make up their minds, nothing or no one can convince them to do otherwise.

No one can stop a desperate man or woman from Nigeria, Ghana, Kenya, Ethiopia, Zimbabwe or South Africa from making the decision to travel to or immigrate to Europe, America, or Australia and begin the journey the way most people do. With little or no money, they will try to go to Libya by crossing the Sahara Desert on foot, and attempt to sneak into Europe without visas through the backdoor by sailing across the Mediterranean Sea in boats that are often not seaworthy.

Many don't make it. They end up drowning when the boats capsize. Those that succeed in landing in Europe are subjected to all kinds of harassment. Many are thrown into detention facilities and are kept there for long periods. Pictures of such tragedies are shown constantly on television screens all over the world.

Likewise, no one can stop anyone from any African country from travelling or immigrating to Dubai, Saudi Arabia or Kuwait only to end up in working under slave-like conditions, unable to get out when they want to.

CHAPTER TWENTY

FUNDRAISING FOR TRAVEL

Do you know how to use your Facebook friends on Facebook, Instagram, Linkedin and other platforms on the internet to get money to travel? If you don't know, here is what you need to know.

Today there are numerous ways to fund anything you want to do, regardless of what it is, where you are or who you are. Some of the ways are tried and true, and have proven to be quite effective in raising funds for people who seek funds for various purposes, while others show a lot of creativity and even wackiness in some cases. But who cares if your fund raising method comes across as unconventional or wacky? So long as it is not illegal or unethical, does not break any laws or regulations, and stays within known guidelines, you are good.

Being able to raise funds for a cause, which happens to be your travel plans, is all that matters. Again, there are so many different ways of going about raising funds for different projects and programs using crowd funding methods that make use of the Internet and social media platforms. All of them are obviously not appropriate for everyone but sometimes, with only a little modification, you might find some fundraising ideas that are perfect for your situation. It takes some researching to find out what will work for you.

Access to funds can be quite a problem for some people who want to travel overseas for one reason or another. They may not have enough money to cover certain necessary expenses that are part of the process. These include but are not limited to obtaining a passport, applying for a visa, buying a ticket and having foreign exchange funds in the currency of the country to which you're travelling or immigrating.

In this chapter, we will look at the latest trends on how people, just like you, can utilize social media, the internet, and other platforms to access and raise funds to do just that. Today, the internet is the new and most dominant platform to use to get money for business, replace the loss of property destroyed in natural disasters and to fund various nonprofit projects. Just about everything, really. You can use social media to get money to pay your travel costs, too. All you have to do is to know how to connect with and interact with your Facebook friends on Facebook, Instagram followers and other social platforms to gain access to sources that can raise funds for you to use to finance your travel.

You can begin by telling your story, why you have felt the need to try that particular method of raising funds for what you are planning to do and why it would make sense for others to support you. You have to be ready and able to upload photos and videos, and add whatever else you think will help to explain why you're trying to raise money. Then, share the page with your social networks via Facebook, Twitter, and email. Most importantly, ask them to share with their friends.

Don't be shy or coy about it. You are not doing anything illegal. All you are doing is using the tools modern technology has provided to raise funds so you can execute your plans of traveling or immigrating overseas. You have absolutely nothing to lose and a whole lot to gain. Who knows? It just might be your luck to find someone who can relate to your story because of their own personal experience or some other reason. They may have the funds to support you and your plans. The important thing is to make the effort.

TEXT TO GIVE

Another method is 'Text to Give' campaigns after major natural disasters. Such campaigns are launched by both well known and not so well known organizations after natural disasters to try to raise funds to help others whose lives have been disrupted and properties destroyed by natural disasters.

Why not consider doing the same for yourself or your organization, that is, if you have some kind of organizational structure to work with. If you don't have any kind of organizational structure to work with, it's easy to do. You can create one and make it serve the purpose of providing you with the legal and administrative framework to operate as a legit non-profit organization or entity. It's not as complicated as you think to create, manage and sustain a nonprofit organization. Many are created and registered every day all over the world.

This is how it works. An organization called the United Performing Arts Fund, Milwaukee, WI, launched its first mobile giving campaign when they decided to use social media to raise funds. During a specified period, anyone with a cell phone could donate $10 to UPAF and its 34 member and affiliate performing arts groups, by texting UPAF to 20222 and then confirming their donation by replying yes to the text message they received back. Donations were tax-deductible, and pledges were billed through the donor's monthly cell phone bill. A one-time donation of $10 was added to the donor's mobile phone bill or deducted from their prepaid balance. It turned out to be a successful fundraising campaign. Anyone can use a similar fundraising approach.

THE BASICS

Again, traveling the world is a dream for many people. While there are ways to do it cheaper and safer than ever with sharing platforms like Airbnb and Couch surfing and more information on budget backpacker travel than could fit an encyclopedia, the cost is still out of reach for most.

But what if you could travel and not spend a dime? Or better yet, what if you could even get paid? Many would jump at the opportunity to experience new cultures, traverse through beautiful landscapes and satisfy their insatiable wanderlust. Luckily there are more ways than ever to travel and get paid. They aren't easy though. Most involve a lot of work, but the opportunities are out there if you want it bad enough. There are many ways for just about anyone to get their travel expenses paid for and even earn some cash in the process. It takes diligence to search, investigate, ask questions and hopefully, find a source that will provide you with the information you need to be able to do it.

Again, you can contact us and we'll help you to gain access to the proper information. Or do it the way most people do these days. Use the Internet to search for answers to your questions by using the ubiquitous Google search engine. You'll be surprised at what you may find.

Research for a travel guidebook

There aren't many professions as romanticized and misunderstood as researching and writing for travel guidebooks such as Lonely Planet and Fodor's. While the job is exhilarating

— jetting you off to hundreds of places to try the local culture, food, and hotels — the reality of the work is a grind.

Most guidebook researchers and writers report having to meet unrealistic deadlines that require them to work 12-to-14-hour days. In addition, seeing the sights is a small part of the job. Researchers and writers must crank out reports and articles, make maps of the areas they visit and engage in extensive, tedious data entry.

Because of tightening budgets and an abundance of 20-somethings willing to do the job for next to nothing, guide writing is hardly a lucrative profession. But you can earn enough to make a living.

In an illuminating *New York Times*' feature about the lives of guidebook writers, Warren St John reveals the cardinal tenet of the job: "Most who do it quickly learn the one hard-and-fast rule of the trade: travel-guide writing is no vacation."

Become an Instagram influencer

Instagram is flooded with "influencers" trying to grow their reach on the platform, but if you are one of the few lucky enough to build a sizeable following, there are opportunities to turn it into serious income.

Twenty-something travel 'grammers' Jack Morris and Lauren Bullen currently parlay the more than three million Instagram followers under the names of their successful travel blogs into travel around the world and a six-figure salary. Morris told Cosmopolitan in an interview that he once earned $9,000 for a single post on Instagram, while Bullen has received $7,500 for one photo. Typically he and Bullen are paid to promote various brands and locations through their feeds.

Even smaller accounts can get some benefits. David Guenther, who runs the Great North Collective, told

Rangefinder Magazine in 2014 he received a free press trip to Alberta, Canada provided that he posted photographs on Instagram.

Of course, most travel Instagrammers end up stuck at a few thousand followers and burning through their savings before they ever cash a check. Best to start building that following before you leave to go anywhere.

Apply for the *New York Times'* 52 Places to go job

Travelling the world and getting to write for one of the most prestigious publications in the world sounds too good to be true right? Wrong. The *New York Times* has announced the creation of a travel correspondent position for the newspaper's annual 52 Places to go feature. The correspondent has to spend a week in each place and write about life on the road. By the time the application deadline for the 2018 post closed, the job had received over 13,000 applicants from all walks of life. The *New York Times* eventually chose Jada Yuan, a veteran New York magazine editor. Better start working on that application. Give it a try. You never know.

Start a side-gig and work remotely

If you have a laptop, the internet, and some skills, there are tons of side-gigs you could pick up to earn cash while you travel. Sites like Fiverr and Upwork are built to make it easy for freelancers to pick up work anywhere, whenever they need it.

Of course, it's a lot easier if you have a track record and marketable skills, like coding, graphic design, writing, translation or editing.

Start taking on side-gigs on freelance websites before you leave and you should be able to build enough of a reputation that you can pick up steady gigs when you need it on the road.

Pretty soon, you'll be earning cash at a beachside cafe in a foreign country.

Start a travel blog

Being a professional travel blogger is a tough gig. While traveling to every sight imaginable is a tantalising part of the job, it takes a lot of work to make it happen.

Most travel bloggers spend a year building their sites, churning out several posts a day and building up a following on social media before they ever see any money from their sites.

Almost all travel bloggers start out by spending their savings just to get it up and running. Even once you've built a following, a network, and ad partnerships, you are running your own business, which means that in addition to traveling and writing, you must handle all the marketing, site growth, and financials. As you can imagine, it's a job that never ends. To make it all work, you have to truly love travel and blogging.

Work as an au pair

An au pair or an extra pair of hands is an international nanny who lives with a family for a set period, taking care of their children in exchange for travel, room, board, and pocket money. It can be a fantastic way to see a new culture from the locals' perspective and make some money. Most au pairs are students or recent graduates, so get in before it's too late.

Many families don't require au pairs to speak the native language, and many even prefer if you speak to their children in English so that they can improve their fluency.

There are websites, such as Au Pair World, that help match people with families.

There is also an extensive application and interview

process. Some organizations pay for travel expenses, living expenses, certain student-loan benefits, and offer allowances.

Write a literary account of your travels

If all else fails (or you are an incredible wordsmith), take a crack at writing the next *Green Hills of Africa*, *Homage to Catalonia* or *The Sun Also Rises*. If the book does well, you could have a cash cow on your hands in the form of royalties and advance checks. Of course, most would-be authors will never see a cent from their travels or literary hard work.

If you have the courage to try, you could end up with the traveling lifestyle and your pick of publications to print your essays and stories.

Crowdfunding is another fundraising method that combines the power of social media with the support of friends and family. It is new, unique and not too difficult to set up. Information on what to do to set up a crowd funding campaign can be obtained easily from the Internet. All you have to do is search for it.

CHAPTER TWENTY ONE

BEGIN WITH AN EXIT STRATEGY TO GO BACK HOME REGARDLESS OF HOW LONG YOU PLAN TO STAY OVERSEAS TO AVOID BECOMING ILLEGAL, STRANDED, TRAPPED AND NOT ABLE TO GO BACK AND FORTHTO YOUR NATIVE COUNTRY

We have already discussed how easy it is for people who travel or immigrate overseas on any kind of visa to get stranded, become illegal and find themselves living the nightmarish life of a wanted person. As soon as their visa runs out, they become illegal aliens in a foreign country and are forced to live like a person on the run from the law, especially if they cannot go to an immigration office to renew their visa or return to their native country,

They lose all their rights and privileges as legal residents in the foreign country they might have entered legally but have overstayed the period the visa allowed them. They cannot leave or reenter if they don't have the 'papers' that permit them to do so. To make matters worse, they are often afraid or scared to go out into the streets, unless it is absolutely necessary. When they venture outside into the streets, to shop, buy groceries, or even to go to work, they make sure they don't go anywhere near the police or any kind of law enforcement, for fear of being caught, detained and deported.

It is certainly not the kind of life anyone would want to live anywhere, but that is the reality of life for those without the proper visas or credentials for foreign nationals in America, Europe, Australia and elsewhere. Yet many find themselves in such situations simply because they have overstayed their visas and have become illegal aliens aa a result.

It is possible to survive and live like a wanted person who has committed a crime and avoid the police or immigration authorities for some time, but sooner or later, their luck runs out. The police or immigration authorities catch up with them, arrest them, put them in jail and finally deport them to their native countries.

You don't want that to happen to you. It is the reason why we are going to discuss the subject of the importance of including plans of returning home to one's native country regardless of how long or brief you plan to stay when you travel or immigrate to a foreign country.

Indeed, returning home has been included to remind readers that it is just as important to plan and prepare for the exit and return home as it is with applying for and being given the right visa. Your plans to travel overseas must have as one of its main components, ideas about what to do or not do to avoid being stranded, becoming illegal or getting trapped. Believe it or not, it's one of the biggest problems most people face when they travel or immigrate.

This is not mere hype. It is real and has claimed many victims. The victims are people who had no idea about what life in a foreign country for a foreigner was all about. All they wanted was to find a way to travel or immigrate to a foreign country by any means necessary; at least, that was what they thought in the beginning. As far as they were concerned, the assumption was that once they succeeded in gaining entry into a foreign country, by whatever means, the rest would follow: they would survive and overcome any problem that would crop up.

Nothing could be further from the truth, but they don't find out until it is too late. The majority of people who travel or immigrate overseas with such a mindset often find themselves facing huge problems they cannot easily solve. They end up without proper visas, cannot go out and look for a job because they don't have the authorization to work, cannot find housing on their own or get a driver's license. They are forced to live like outlaws, hiding from the authorities and constantly on the run. Again, you don't want that to happen to you when you travel or immigrate overseas.

HOW THE PROCESS OF BECOMING ILLEGAL BEGINS IN THEIR NATIVE COUNTRIES WITH A WRONG VISA

The desperation of immigrants, particularly from Africa, Asia, the Caribbean, the Middle East and other Third World countries as they scramble to get to America, Europe, Australia and elsewhere has been well documented. They will do everything possible to travel overseas or immigrate, according to media reports. Regardless of how long the journey takes, the hazards and obstacles to be faced, and quite often the exorbitant fees charged by smugglers and criminals, they manage to find the means, the will power and the energy to do it. These include those willing to travel without making sure that the visas they are travelling with would not expire when they are not yet ready to return home. In other words, they don't really care about the kind of visa they are traveling or immigrating with.

In as much as we would like to encourage prospective travelers and immigrants to foreign countries to make every effort to obtain proper visas, there's the likelihood that many would grab whatever chance comes their way to leave their naïve countries. It simply means that the person involved is setting himself or herself up to become illegal, trapped and miserable in an overseas country. What many don't know is what actually happens to those who manage to enter legally, overstay their visas and become illegal as a result. They usually encounter very serious problems that end up in deportation. Only a few lucky ones succeed in making the transition from illegal to legal residents.

There is a bigger problem, again for those who manage to enter legally, but become illegal as a result of overstaying their visas.

BEGINNING OF THE PROBLEM IS NOT KNOWING ANYTHING ABOUT THE FOREIGN COUNTRY YOU ARE TRAVELING OR IMMIGRATING TO

The majority of people who have recently arrived or immigrated to a foreign country usually have little or no knowledge about such things as retirement, pension plans and other benefits in those foreign countries. Also, many have to deal with other issues that disqualify them from receiving any kind of benefits including the all-important retirement benefits.

One of the main problems cited above is not having proper and valid documents. Without proper documents, a large number are forced to work for long periods for companies that don't have retirement and pension plans and end up contributing little or nothing to the social security and retirement systems that are set up to take care of those who contribute to it. Consequently, they don't qualify to receive social security benefits when they reach retirement age, if they are lucky to live there long enough to reach retirement age. Others may be self-employed in businesses they own that don't generate enough funds to be make it possible for them to save for retirement or pay into a pension and retirement program on their own.

At this point however, which is the early part of their stay overseas, most don't see any need to think about the future, certainly not in terms of what they have to do to take care of their needs when they are not able to work as a result of old age, senility or poor health. The last things they think about are retirement and pension. They might have other more pressing problems to deal with that may include trying to get their 'papers' and becoming legal residents.

If they think about pension and retirement, it is relation to their ultimate goal of being able to accomplish the mission that took them out of their native countries in the first place: to get a job, save as much as they can and go back home when they have what they need. It all boils down to one word: funds.

We have stated elsewhere that it is possible to take steps to avoid becoming a victim. And it's all about knowing what has to be done to put pension and retirement plans in place that will kick in when health and age related issues make it impossible to continue to work. The following suggestions have been made.

- Include retirement and pension in all plans. Ask yourself questions about how, when and where you would want to retire and what you'll have to do to make sure you can retire when it is time to do so, and have enough funds or access to resources to be able to live a reasonably decent lifestyle where you are or back home in your native country. Never mind the fact that you are young or newly arrived. The majority of immigrants who are stuck in America, Europe, Australia and elsewhere almost always made the mistake of thinking they didn't need to make retirement plans for the future that included returning home.

- Prepare yourself to be able to do what it takes to contribute to social security or any other retirement and pension plans in the country in which you find yourself. Bear in mind that you live in a society that may not assume full responsibility for your safety and wellbeing when you are too old, weak, senile and unable to work. Ask questions and you will get the answers. Don't just assume that what you know is enough. Usually, it's not.

- Be realistic about what you can do to lay the foundation for you to return home. If your plans include having a house built or a business started in your native country, ask yourself if you are you in a position to do it before you retire. If not, what can you do to make it happen sooner rather than later?

- Make every effort to pursue higher education in a field that will gain you professional qualifications. That will prepare you to qualify to get a job that pays more than the average wage in addition to being able to contribute to a pension and retirement program. Regardless, a job that pays good money puts you in a better position to be able to save towards retirement and pension on your own, if you decide to go that route. If you have plans to build a home or start a business back home in your native country, like most people, a job that pays good money will certainly help to reach that goal faster.

CONCLUSION

No matter where you live, which part of the world you come from or who you are, your life is impacted in one way or another, directly or indirectly by the immigration process and travel related issues. More than likely one or more of your neighbors, colleagues at work, business associates, spouse, boyfriend or girlfriend might be an immigrant or have relatives who are immigrants.

It is not surprising therefore that immigration, migration and travel related issues are recurrent themes in the global media, and lately, on social media and have become the hottest topic in global politics in part because of the impact they have on all aspects of an individual and society's life.

Emigration, migration, immigration, foreign travel and tourism; they basically revolve around one thing: the visa. It is the key element in international travel and immigration and plays a major role when it comes to leaving familiar surroundings of your native country for a strange new place where you may not know anyone, where you have to adjust to a new and different culture, lifestyle, foods and eating habits, religion, politics, etc. Question is: why do some succeed, while others fail?

The answer is simple: how you go about it. Like everything else, it's all in the planning. It has to be approached in pretty much the same way as one would when it comes to any kind of undertaking that involves funds, time and other people. It's all about having the right information, knowing what to expect, having an idea about what to do, when to do it, how to go about doing it and with whom. Books have been written about the process, by people describing themselves as experts and claiming to have answers to questions on the subject. They advertise their services all over the place.

The bottom line is; you have to do what it takes, know what is involved and make a real and concerted effort to meet the requirements, to the best of your ability. Hopefully, what you've read in these pages has not discouraged you from pursuing your plans to travel or immigrate to a foreign country. If anything, we hope that it has provided you with information and insight that will help you to reach your goal of traveling to an overseas country.

QUESTIONNAIRE FOR THOSE PLANNING TO TRAVEL OR IMMIGRATE TO A FOREIGN COUNTRY

Answer the following questions as truthfully as you can.

1. What makes you think you are prepared to immigrate to another country?

ANSWER

Pick one of the following answers.

a. I am counting on friends and relatives to help me out when I get there.

b. Friends and relatives have promised to take care of me while I look for a job.

c. I hope to enter into a school once I get there.

d. I have already made specific arrangements to support myself in school or wait to get a job.

2. What do you plan to do when you arrive in the new country?

ANSWER

a. Hope to find a job.

b. Expect to pursue higher education.

c. Begin a program of study in a school in which I am already enrolled or I already have a job.

d. My uncle will help me find me a job.

3. What do you know about the new country: the culture, the politics, the racial situation, etc?

ANSWER

a. Very little.

b. I know a lot.

c. I know about the culture, the politics, the racial situation and so forth.

d. I know as much about that country as I know about my own country.

4. What do you know about the laws and regulations covering employment, hiring, education, and housing for foreigners in the country to which you are traveling or immigrating?

ANSWER

a. I know nothing about the laws and regulations governing employment, housing, education, but I am the kind of person who learns fast.

b. I know exactly what documents I have to possess in order to be able to go and look for a job, a house, go to school, etc.

c. I believe what my friends have said, that there is a job, school, and a house for everybody who can get the visa to travel to that country.

d. I never had a problem finding a job, a house, or a school in my country, and don't expect to have any problems in another country.

5. What was the source of most of the information you have about the new country?

ANSWER

a. Books, newspapers, magazines, brochures.

b. Films, movies, television, pictures.

c. People from my country that have traveled to that country.

d. Natives of the country where I plan to immigrate.

6. Do you have written statements from people, schools, and prospective employers in the country to which you are traveling or immigrating or are you assuming that you will get help from people who have promised to help you?

ANSWER

a. I have no written or formal documents.

b. I am in possession of forms of admission to an educational institution, letter of employment from the organization that will employ me.

c. I have no letters from relatives and friends; I believe in the promises they have made.

d. In my culture, we take care of each other, so I believe my friends and relatives will take care of me.

7. What makes you believe that friends and relatives will keep promises they make?

ANSWER

a. They have kept all the promises they made in the past.

b. Friends and relatives rely on each other in our culture.

c. It is part of our culture to take care of each other.

d. I shall plan on being able to continue with or without the help of friends and relatives

8. What contingency plans do you have should friends and relatives fail to keep promises?

ANSWER

a. I have no contingency plans.

b. I don't see the need to make any plans besides those arranged with friends and relatives.

c. I'll wait to see what happens.

d. I am fully prepared with alternative plans should the worse happen.

9. Are you prepared to return home, if you find the immigrant life different from what you thought?

ANSWER

a. No.

b. Too soon to return home.

c. I'll try my best to figure out a way to continue the immigrant life.

d. I'll return to my native country.

10. Are you sacrificing everything in order to travel overseas?

ANSWER

a. No.

b. I'm taking a leave of absence from my job.

c. Yes, I am risking everything, hoping that everything will turn out well.

d. I know I'll succeed. If others have done it, so can I.

ANSWERS

None of the responses provided above can be considered as wrong, incorrect, bad or inappropriate; nor can any one be regarded as the perfect answer. Whatever response you choose serves to give an indication of the extent to which you are prepared, informed, and ready to deal with life in a different country as an immigrant. In other words, the quiz has been designed to assess weaknesses and strengths and provide some insight into the immigrant experience. The points range from ten to two. Add all the points and the total figure represents the score. The higher the score, the better prepared you are to deal with life as an immigrant in making the transition from the old lifestyle to the new, adjusting to a new environment and culture, etc.

POINTS

| 10 | 8 | 6 | 2 |

Question 1

1	D	C	B	A
2	C	B	A	D
3	C	D	B	A
4	B	C	D	A
5	D	C	B	A
6	B	D	C	A
7	D	A	B	C
8	D	C	B	A
9	C	B	D	A
10	B	D	C	A

CONCLUSION

If you scored between 100 and 80 points, it is a strong indication that you have a fairly good understanding of what is involved in traveling and immigrating to an overseas country. You have an idea of what to expect, you are prepared to deal with it, and stand a good chance of making the transition without difficulty. 80 to 60 points suggest that you have some understanding of the process, but may not be in possession of everything you need to know to be better prepared to deal with it. 60 to 40 points is an indication that you need to be more informed about the process, and need to find out what to expect, what problems to anticipate, etc. 40 to 20 points most certainly calls for the individual to take some time to be better informed, educated and prepared in all aspects of the process. Talk to people who have traveled overseas before and experienced the immigrant life. More than likely, they will be glad to answer all your questions.

If you are interested in a more detailed response and finding out more about your prospects, based on the responses you have given, send email to internationaltravelassociates@gmail.com.

REQUEST FOR MORE INFORMATION

We encourage readers to let us know if they are interested in receiving more information about travel and immigration-related issues discussed in this book. We know it doesn't stop here. There is a lot more to it than what we have discussed in this book. The important thing is the information and resources are available, and it can be done. All you need is the know-how and the ability to prepare to provide the information and documents needed to show that you know what is involved and know what you need to do. If you are interested in receiving more information, send email to internationaltravelassociates@gmail.com.

International Travel Associates
International Travel Affiliates

[Worldwide Immigrants Network: WIN]

We encourage you to become an affiliate or an associate of our global travel group above and enjoy the following benefits.

Become part of a global network of men and women who share information, ideas, and knowledge about their travel and immigrant experiences in different countries with different cultures.

Connect and interact with people like you who have read this book, who need or have more information and are willing to network with others with similar objectives and goals. Most importantly, you will join a worldwide group of men and women like you who want to travel and immigrate and are willing to network with you and others to make it happen.

This is not like your average friendship club that simply arranges for people to meet. We go one step further. We make it possible for people to meet not just to become Facebook and social media friends, but to learn about each other's culture, history, etc.

Our goal is to establish a common forum for the exchange of ideas, information and data on the subject of this book, traveling and immigrating overseas

Membership is open to men and women interested in interacting with likeminded individuals; no age limit. Everyone seeking to connect with someone from another country or another culture is welcome to join, no matter how young or old.

Send email to interrnationaltravelassociates@gmail.com

This book focuses on the subject of immigrants that have been trapped in foreign countries, what causes it and what to do to avoid becoming a victim. Get a copy today on www.amazon.com

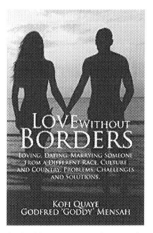

The problems and challenges in relationships and marriages between people from different countries, races, and cultures are discussed and analyzed in this book with suggestions on solutions for those involved. Available on www.amazon.com